Praise for *The Janitor*

"Take a few minutes and devour this little book by Todd Hopkins and Ray Hilbert. It's going to be a motivational classic, and you'll be in on the first wave of inspired readers."

>   —**Pat Williams,** Senior Vice President, Orlando Magic; and Author, *The Warrior Within*

"Ray Hilbert and Todd Hopkins have hit a grand slam home run with *The Janitor*. This is a must-read for anyone who desires to dramatically impact lives in the workplace. This book will change hearts, reshape attitudes, and truly provoke thought. Don't waste a minute thinking about reading this book; just grab it and get started. Before you know it, you will be recommending it to a friend."

>   —**Mark Cress**, President and CEO, Corporate Chaplains of America, Inc.

"Wow—after I stopped sobbing and cleared my eyes, I reflected on what Steve Jobs, founder of Apple, shared with us years ago when he said the key to success is to 'follow your heart using your head.' Todd and Ray's book so clearly puts the critical 'heart' side back into your business and your life. Read this book and weep with joy as their six directives breathe new life into *you*, your business, and your personal relationships."

>   —**Verne Harnish,** Founder, Young Entrepreneurs' Organization; and CEO, Gazelles, Inc.

"I wish I would have read this book before I retired. I would have done a lot of things differently."

>   —**John McBeath,** Retired Arvins executive

"More often than I can recall, conventional wisdom appears tainted if not clearly wrong. Isn't it true that we often find pearls of wisdom in the most unusual places and circumstances? You will be glued to the pages of *The Janitor* as Bob provides a gift of wisdom to a CEO in need. *The Janitor* is testimony to the 'gift of giving' that 'keeps on giving.'

—**Jim Gleed,** TEC Chairman, Pensacola, FL

"What a fantastic book! I started reading it while eating lunch. Needless to say, I had a long lunch today because I could not put the book down until I finished it two hours later. I thoroughly enjoyed reading it. I guarantee that anyone who reads this book will take away the principles and apply them to their own lives."

—**Donald L. Pottieger Sr.,** CBSE, Chairman, FMI Services Group, Inc.

"In *The Janitor*, Todd and Ray mix a solid blend of faith with practical business and life advice."

—**Tom Salonek,** CEO, Intertech

"*The Janitor* is a great read; it is one of those books that business leaders can easily relate to and can immediately put to use. This will be an encouragement for any business leader who struggles to maintain a proper balance between business, family, church, and community; also, it is a great tool to use to encourage others."

—**Dennis Richards,** President, Puritan Cleaning Professionals

"I found *The Janitor* to be an easy read, but full of insight and inspiration. Alice's directives remind us not only as business owners but also as individuals that on occasion we all should reassess the direction our lives are taking and who or what might be influencing the decisions we make on a day-to-day basis. I believe anyone who chooses to follow these directives will realize how important the family should be and make it a priority second only to God in setting personal goals and making business and individual decisions."

—**Lee Medley,** Attorney-at-Law

"This book speaks to *real* life, family, and faith. Todd and Ray have captured what we have been privileged to witness close up and personal within the Office Pride system. May God bless you as you focus your life and look to get a better view of the *real* 'Janitor Bob' in you."

—**Mark and Brian Wages,** Office Pride Area Developers

"This is a very enjoyable and must-read parable that reveals to entrepreneurs how to be successful in business without sacrificing their personal lives."

—**Jeffrey J. Fox,** Best-Selling Author, *Secrets of Great Rainmakers*

"Todd and Ray have captured in *The Janitor* the inevitable 'tyranny of the urgent' that so often consumes the average business owner/manager. Through the help of Bob's six directives, one can reestablish those priorities in life too often taken for granted."

—**Jeff Roush,** VP and General Manager, Tom Roush Lincoln/Mercury/Mazda, Westfield, IN

"While *The Janitor* is written in a light-hearted style, the principles offered in this book are not light at all. These principles make for very serious business. Readers will be encouraged to refocus their energies and efforts on what truly matters . . . the opportunities to build relationships. The mission of changing people's lives is no longer just for churches and other nonprofit organizations. Hopkins and Hilbert effectively remind each one of us to consider this greater sense of mission."

—**Larry W. Rottmeyer, PhD,** Chair, MBA Program, Taylor University

"Ray and Todd have hit it out of the park with this book. It is incisive, practical, and grabs you at the heart level. You'll find yourself taken into the story and come out with tremendous and powerful insights."

—**Dr. Ron Jenson,** Cofounder, Future Achievement International; Author; Speaker; and Life Coach

"*The Janitor*'s simple 'directives' are a wake-up call for men who are too busy to realize their God-given purpose. I was encouraged to slow my pace and focus more on things of eternal importance. It is a must-read for the pathologically busy men of our generation!"

—**Dr. Stephen P. Hadley,** Group Vice President, VCA Animal Hospitals, Los Angeles, CA

"As compelling a book as I've ever read. I couldn't put it down—read the complete book in one day. I believe this book will speak to every aspiring executive who desires to be truly successful in life as well as at work. The six directives are practical, applicable, and definitely real-life stuff."

—**Kyle De Fur,** FACHE, President, Saint John's Health System

"This book has the power to change your life! As a professional athlete, I always had to remain focused on the basic fundamentals of my sport to enjoy success. *The Janitor* will give you all the basics you need to succeed in business and in all the important areas of your life."

—**Derek Daly,** Formula One Race Driver; Motor Sports Television Analyst; and Founder, Motorvation Performance Company

"*The Janitor* is a great story of how God sends the right people into our lives at the right time, even if the person He sends to us is the janitor. Thank God!"

—**John S. Ezzo,** CBSE, CEO, New Image Enterprises LLC; and President, BSCAI

THE JANITOR

How an Unexpected Friendship
Transformed a CEO and His Company

TODD HOPKINS & RAY HILBERT

THOMAS NELSON
Since 1798

NASHVILLE   DALLAS   MEXICO CITY   RIO DE JANEIRO

Published in Nashville, TN by Thomas Nelson. Thomas Nelson is a registered trademark of Thomas Nelson, Inc.

Thomas Nelson, Inc. titles may be purchased in bulk for educational, business, fund-raising, or sales promotional use. For information, please e-mail SpecialMarkets@ThomasNelson.com.

ISBN-13: 978-1-59555-327-0 (tradepaper)

Library of Congress Cataloging-in-Publication Data

Hopkins, Todd.
  The janitor : how an unexpected friendship transformed a CEO and his company / Todd Hopkins and Ray Hilbert.
      p. cm.
  ISBN-13: 978-0-7852-2319-1 (hardcover)
  1. Businessmen—Religious life. 2. Success in business. I. Hilbert, Ray. II. Title.
BV4596.B8H67 2007
248.8'8—dc22

                                        2006037785

Printed in the United States of America
10 11 12 13 RRD 5 4 3 2 1

**To all the business leaders,
their spouses, and Janitor Bobs in the world**

INTRODUCTION

B ob Tidwell slapped his knees and stood up from the chair in a motion quite lithe for a man of his age. He tucked the pencil stub back in the spiral of his small notebook, picked up his cup, tea bag, and spoon from the table, and wiped the table clean with a paper towel and spray cleaner. He tossed the tea bag in the garbage, then washed the cup and spoon with plenty of suds and placed them on the drying rack next to the sink in the break room of the offices of Triple A Enterprises.

"There!" he said, as if admiring a garden he had just finished trimming.

As he walked out of the break room down the corridor, he admired a line of large framed photographs displaying groups of Triple A employees posing proudly next to their line of metal fabricated products. Some of the objects Bob didn't recognize; they looked like parts that would go into making some kind of machinery, but others were truly impressive, like the photo of the customized ornamental stair railings fitted in the opulent lobby of the new modern-art museum. The image included a group of five men in hard hats and shirts bearing the company logo, smiling for the camera. They looked quite happy about their achievement.

Bob started singing an aria from his favorite opera, filling in the words he didn't remember with a bom-ba-bom until he could get back to the part where he knew the lyrics. Sometimes the memory of the original music in his head was so beautiful that Bob became misty-eyed. Seeing that the light was still on at this late hour in the office of the CEO, Bob automatically thought of Puccini's aria "No One Sleeps" from the opera *Turandot*.

"Nessun dorma, nessun doooorma," he sang as he pushed the neat cart that organized all his cleaning implements, the tools of his trade.

"Tu pure, o Principessa, Nella tua fredda staaaaanza," he continued as he wiped and dusted the desks and computers with a confident hand.

"Guardi le stelle, Che tremano d'amore." He put his hand to his heart. "E di speraaaanza."

Suddenly a voice broke Bob's concentration.

"You have a good voice!" the CEO said, standing at his doorway.

"I'm sorry. Did I disturb you?" asked Bob politely.

"No, actually I loved it. You sounded happy. Is it an

opera?" he asked as he leaned his trim, well-dressed figure against the door frame.

"Yes, Puccini."

"What do the words mean?"

"Oh, well, it's in Italian. I'm not sure I'll get it right, but it goes something like:

"No one sleeps, no one sleeps . . .
Even you, O Princess,
In your cold room,
Watch the stars,
That tremble with love
And with hope."*

The CEO smiled. "Sounds like me, in my cold room, still awake, except I'm not a princess," he said.

"Yeah, and the room is not cold," Bob said with a chuckle.

"And the stars don't hold any hope for me." The CEO looked down at his shoes.

Bob was taken aback by such a personal revelation from someone whom he had just seen in passing on Monday evenings when he cleaned the Triple A office.

---

* The Italian libretto of *Turandot* is copyright 1926 by G. Ricordi & Co. The translation is provided by Mark D. Lew, copyright © 1997. More information can be found at http://home.earthlink.net/~markdlew/comm/turandot.htm.

"I'm sorry to hear that. I don't mean to invade your privacy but . . ." Bob hesitated. Although this man looked so young, he was still the boss.

"Yeah, I should be getting home anyway. I can't believe how late it is." The handsome man shrugged and turned back inside his office.

Bob continued his rhythmic cleaning and wiping. On one of the computer keyboards, he found a chocolate with a Post-it Note. It read, "Bob, thank-you for cleaning my desk in spite of the mess I left behind last Monday. You are an angel. Becky." Bob put the chocolate in his shirt pocket and smiled. Becky was the executive assistant to the CEO. She had left quite a mess, and Bob had spent an extra ten minutes to clean her desk and then to make sure that he put everything back exactly in its place. He had left a Post-it for Becky saying that he hoped he hadn't disturbed her notes. Bob just knew her through the wedding picture on her desk, because Becky was long gone by the time he started cleaning. She looked friendly, her smile filled with light, and Bob thought that her husband must be a lucky man.

The light went out in the CEO's office, and the young man waved a polite good-bye to Bob as he stepped into the elevator. Bob felt a little sad for him.

I wonder what makes a young, handsome man, owner of such a successful company, think that there is no hope?

He broke into the next line of Puccini's aria at the top of his voice now that he was alone.

"Ma il mio mistero è chiuso in me . . ."

How appropriate, Bob thought of the translation: *But my secret is hidden within me.*

CHAPTER ONE

On the following two Mondays, Bob noticed that the light was still on in the young CEO's office, but he made it a point not to disturb the busy man. He waited until the CEO left to clean the elegant corner office. This Monday, Bob was just starting to prepare his cup of green tea before he launched into his well-choreographed cleaning routine that took him through the entire office, top to bottom, nonstop in two hours flat. After retiring from his prosperous business career, Bob had taken this job as a way to get out of the house and stay active while doing something useful at the same time.

Bob turned the work almost into a fitness circuit. He found that he really enjoyed the manual work; it freed up his mind to give shape to his thoughts. Ever since Alice died two years ago, evenings were the hardest time for him because that was when they would usually sit down and talk about the events of the day. It was the little things that Bob missed the most about Alice—the smell of her hair on the pillow, her way of folding his paper in the morning so that he would see the comics before the news (reading bad news first thing in the morning has to be bad for your heart, she would say). She was kind, his Alice; she was smart and very, very kind. They had a sweet, long life together and three beautiful children who had produced the most wonderful gift time can bring—three healthy, ebullient grandchildren.

As he waited for the water to boil, Bob made some notes in the little spiral orange notebook that he carried everywhere. The door opened behind him, and the young CEO came in, carrying an empty mug.

"Good evening, Mr. Kimbrough," Bob said.

"Please call me Roger. I'm sorry, I never caught your name," the young man replied.

"Bob Tidwell," Bob said with a nod, getting up to pour his tea.

"What are you writing, Bob?"

"Oh, it's just a habit of mine. I keep writing the same notes over and over, trying to get them perfect. I've been at it for two years." Bob signaled to Roger's empty mug. "Can I get you something?"

"I'll do it. You sit down and tell me more about opera. What do you drink?"

Bob was amused at the role reversal. "Green tea. It's good for you."

"Okay. I'll have the same then."

Bob sat down, and Roger poured two steaming mugs of green tea and handed one to Bob. He sat down across the table and rubbed the bridge of his nose.

"Tired?" Bob asked.

"Boy, I'm bushed," he said.

"I noticed that you often work late," Bob ventured.

"Often is not the word. Always is more like it. I practically live in this office. I used to enjoy it so much."

"But you don't anymore?"

"I don't know. It feels like I'm living to work. I get home, and my wife and girls are already asleep. On weekends I always have some function to go to, or I spend half my time on the phone. I don't get to spend any time with them."

"That's a shame. They grow so fast," Bob observed.

"Do you have kids?" Roger asked.

"Yep. Two sons and a daughter. All grown now, and I have three grandchildren."

"Got pictures?"

"Of course. You'll be sorry you asked!" Bob took out his wallet, which had a foldout with one picture each for all the family members. The first one was Alice.

"Is that your wife?"

"Yes, that's Alice. She passed away two years ago." Bob tightened his lips.

"I'm sorry," Roger said.

"Thank-you. I miss her every day. She is the love of my life. We were very happy together."

"Really? Not many people can say that these days." Roger seemed surprised.

"Absolutely. Alice was a formidable woman. She was a great partner, a good mother, and a very wise person. She's the one who got me hooked on opera and classical music. She was interested in everything. She enjoyed cooking exotic meals for our friends, and she made even the simplest thing beautiful. She taught me how to live. That's why I'm writing these notes. I'm trying to remember her six directives for living a happy life both at home and at work, and I keep correcting them to get them exactly right."

"That sounds interesting. Why six?" Roger was intrigued.

"I have no idea! You'd have to ask Alice." Bob chuckled with glee. "But I can tell you that they work."

"Can I read the six directives?" Roger asked, pointing at the little orange notebook.

"Oh, no, I'm not even close to getting them right yet," Bob replied, tucking the little orange notebook back in his shirt pocket.

"Come on, Bob," Roger teased him, "I can use some help."

"Really?" Bob thought a moment. "Are you really interested?"

"Well, I figure that at the rate I'm going, either my wife will leave me and take the kids and half my earthly belongings with her, or even worse, I'll have a premature heart attack and pop my clogs right here in this office."

"That bad?" Bob asked in a softer voice.

"Let me give you an example of how my life goes. It was my wife's thirtieth birthday last week," Roger said. "I promised we would have a romantic dinner, just the two of us. I even made reservations. Then I forgot. I got home, and she was already asleep. There was a huge bunch of flowers on the entrance table, with a card signed by me. Except it was not sent by me. Becky, my assistant, had remembered and sent it in my name. She had also tried to remind me, but my mobile phone was turned off."

Roger continued. "I was in the middle of closing a deal with a big Chinese client. I had been working on it for months. The meeting was scheduled for the day before, but the flight of the Chinese reps got canceled, so they arrived a day late. I had to change all my meetings at the last minute, it was a mad rush, and they were leaving the same night for their next stop. I took them out to dinner, with a translator, and ended up signing the papers at the airport, right before they boarded their flight. Everything moved so fast. I remember driving home in my sleek luxury car, feeling like Superman. Then when I saw the flowers and realized I had forgotten my wife's birthday, I felt like I couldn't breathe. My wife has not spoken to me since. So there you have it, Bob. I am a cockroach."

"Hardly," Bob said.

"What do you mean?"

"To me, it sounds like you are very human, and you are just working too hard."

"I don't know why I'm doing this anymore. My home has turned into a battlefield. I sometimes feel like I'm living with a stranger, who just keeps me around to pay off the credit cards."

"Oh, boy, I think you do need the six directives." Bob thought a moment and reached a decision. "I tell you what. You give me a week, and I'll get the first one ready for you next Monday. I bet you that in six weeks, one directive at a time, you can turn your life around and enjoy both your family and your work again."

"I don't mean to be rude, Bob, but that right now sounds impossible."

"I thought you wanted to read the six directives a minute ago?" Bob wagged the little orange notebook in the air.

"All right. You have me intrigued now. What do I have to do?" asked Roger, smiling for the first time.

"That's better." Bob smiled back. "You just make me a cup of green tea on Monday evening, and I'll come by half an hour early to share the notes with you. But you have to give me time to get them right, so only one directive per week. Deal?"

"Deal." Then pointing to the empty tea mug, Roger added, "By the way, that tea better be good for you. Man, that stuff is bitter!"

They both broke out in a relaxed chuckle as they went back to their jobs, Bob to clean the office and Roger to run it.

CHAPTER **TWO**

Roger Kimbrough let himself in through the kitchen door to a house that was still, silent, and dark. On the kitchen counter, there was a platter covered in plastic wrap, with a note written in an unsteady scribble. It read *Daddy's Dinner* and was signed *Becca*. Roger was more tired than hungry, but popped the plate in the microwave anyway. He looked at the note one more time and noticed something written on the other side. It was a picture of a big heart encircling four stick figures—two big ones for Mom and Dad and two small ones for the girls. Roger smiled at Becca's signature. Their elder daughter, Sarah, was only two when Rebecca was born. The closest that little Sarah could bring herself to pronounce her baby sister's name was *Becca*, and the name stuck—even though Rebecca was now five and Sarah seven.

I bet that's the way a lot of nicknames are formed. Older brothers and sisters mispronouncing their siblings' names.

Roger reflected on how Becca could now write a note to

her daddy. She had grown up so quickly. The last couple of years were a blur. It seemed that she had skipped directly from cradle to play school. But she was still very definitely the baby of the house, chatting incessantly about her friends at school or the amazing adventures of her invisible friend, Chuck. Sarah, on the other hand, had developed a quiet self-assuredness and was growing up into a competent young girl. She gave no trouble at school and always went to bed on time. Roger worried more about Sarah.

The beep of the microwave seemed unduly loud in contrast to the quiet kitchen. Roger took his dinner out of the microwave. Grilled chicken, corn, and spinach. Darlene was a good cook; she prepared thoughtful, healthy meals. The chicken had probably been very tasty at some point, but Roger had left it in the microwave too long, and it had turned into a rubbery mound. He poured a tall glass of water and swallowed two aspirin tablets to loosen his stiff neck. He finished his dinner and slipped the dirty plate in the dishwasher. He realized too late that the dishwasher had just finished the cleaning cycle and his dirty plate had splattered food all over the clean dishes. He recognized the girls' colorful plates, decorated with the letters of the alphabet, their drinking cups, and the other dishes, probably from Darlene's dinner. He felt a pang of sadness. His dirty plate now seemed out of place with all the neat and clean dishes from the family meal that he had missed. He seemed to be going against the current of the house.

At the bottom of the stairs, Roger removed his shoes so he wouldn't wake the girls, and he climbed quietly up to their room. With the light coming in from the half-opened door, he could make out Becca's mass of blonde curls on her pillow. She looked so tiny now that she had graduated to a proper twin-size bed. Sarah, on the other bed, was completely covered under the duvet. Roger kissed Becca and breathed in the familiar smell of apple-scented shampoo in her hair, and then he reached over to kiss Sarah.

"I heard the car," Sarah said in a sleepy voice.

"I'm sorry, I didn't mean to wake you," Roger said.

"Did you find your dinner?" she asked, sounding like a proper hostess.

"Yes, sweetheart, thank-you. It was delicious," Roger lied. "Go back to sleep now. I love you."

"Luvya," Sarah muttered as she sank deeper into her pillow.

Roger slipped into the master bedroom without turning on the light. Darlene had left the bathroom light on for him. He undressed quietly and got into bed, too tired to sleep. Numbers and snippets of conversations and e-mails ran through his head; he was unable to turn off the business side of his brain. If he didn't go to sleep soon, he would have trouble getting up in the morning, and with the state of things at work, that was a luxury he could not afford. He set the alarm for 6:00 a.m. and went to the bathroom and took one of Darlene's sleeping pills to help him unwind. He lay in bed awake for a long time, staring at the blue reflection of the numbers on the digital alarm clock. He could hear Darlene's breathing in and out at even intervals.

A piercing scream shattered the quiet house. One of the girls was crying at the top of her lungs. Darlene jumped from bed and went straight to the girls' room. Roger followed close behind. As he reached the room, Darlene was hugging Sarah close to her chest and soothing her. Sarah was shaking with sobs and was drenched in sweat.

"What's wrong?" Roger asked.

"Just a bad dream," said Darlene. "Shhhhh, honey. It's okay." She rocked Sarah to help the little girl calm down and spoke again to her husband: "Go back to bed, Roger. She's okay."

"Are you sure?" Roger asked, already feeling the effects of the pill.

"Yes, she'll settle down faster if we don't make a fuss." Darlene's voice sounded mechanical.

Roger went back to bed, and Darlene followed a few minutes later.

"Is Sarah okay?" he asked.

"No, she's not okay. She's been waking up with horrible

nightmares these last three nights." Darlene's tone was chilly. "You haven't noticed because you are seldom home."

"What do you think is bothering her?" he asked.

"I don't know. When she wakes up in the morning, she says she doesn't remember the bad dreams," Darlene said.

"Should we take her to the doctor?" Roger asked.

"Should 'we' . . . meaning should 'I' take her?" Darlene said, her tone escalating in sarcasm.

She fluffed her pillow a little too vigorously.

"Darlene, you know I'm too busy. I just have to rely on you for these things." Roger evaded the question.

"Yes," Darlene said, with an impatient edge in her voice, "you have to rely on me. Of course you have to rely on me. Good thing I can be relied on!"

A silence followed as Roger, under the effects of the sleeping pill, was finding it hard to stay focused.

"What is that supposed to mean," asked Roger, "that I am not reliable? Is that what you're trying to say?"

"I'm not trying to say anything other than what I'm saying," answered Darlene.

"Huh?" Roger mumbled.

"Fine. I'll try to make an appointment with Dr. Gordon," Darlene said, getting back into bed.

"Thanks for dinner, by the way. I'm sorry I was late," Roger said by way of a peace offering.

"The girls waited for you until their heads were falling on their plates," Darlene said in a voice of steel and ice.

"I know. I got tied up, and then I got into this strange conversation with the janitor," Roger started to explain.

Darlene cut him off. "I don't need an explanation, Roger."

"I said I was sorry," Roger repeated. "It's my work, Darlene. You know it."

"I don't care if you are sorry or not. I am not interested in excuses anymore. I hope you know what you are doing."

"I'm trying, Darlene. I just can't cope with everything that's going on."

"I'm not going to tell you what you should or shouldn't do, Roger. Day after day I have been hoping that you will come to your senses. I've cried more tears than I ever thought I had. I have spent hours preparing a meal, and then I've waited night after night, staring at your food getting cold on the plate. With every passing car I keep thinking that it's you. But it isn't. This conversation ended for me weeks ago. I am exhausted. I don't know if you can't see it or if you won't see it. You checked yourself out of this family a long time ago. What I am saying now is that I don't want to have the same argument over and over. I am tired of talking to a brick wall."

"I am not a brick wall. I am doing my best, and it's just never good enough for you," Roger replied.

"I refuse to have this conversation again, Roger. I am tired, and I need to get some sleep," Darlene said with finality and turned off the light.

Roger dozed off under the effects of the medication, falling into a fitful sleep until the alarm screeched him back to consciousness. He got up, showered, dressed, and dashed out the door while Darlene and the girls were still asleep. He got to his office before anyone else, so he turned on the lights and started a pot of coffee.

Maybe it is not even worth it to drive all this way; soon I'll just have to set up a foldout bed right here in this office.

CHAPTER THREE

Roger looked at the clock on his computer screen. It was almost time for his meeting with Janitor Bob. The week had zoomed by like a flash, and today he was even more exhausted than he was last Monday when he first met Bob. After a weekend of playing host to the executives from Crockett Steel, Roger's top customer, over golf, cocktails, and dinner, he was completely drained. He was now trying to concentrate on the same e-mail he had been attempting to draft since morning. Every time he started on it, either the phone rang or one of his employees came in with an urgent problem. Bob would have to wait. He just had to finish this e-mail.

Roger walked quickly to the break room and found Bob already fixing two mugs of green tea.

"Hey, Roger, how have you been?" Bob asked with a smile.

"I've been better," Roger huffed. "Listen, Bob, about our appointment today . . ."

"You're too busy, I know," Bob said.

"Yes, I just have to finish this letter, and I've been interrupted a thousand times today. I'm sorry. Maybe next week?"

"Sure. Take the tea with you, though." Bob handed him a steaming mug.

"The bitter stuff, huh?" Roger smiled for the first time in days.

Directive 1: Recharge versus discharge

"Yep. There are some things in life that are bitter to swallow but actually make you stronger." Bob winked.

"You're not talking about the green tea, right?" Roger guessed.

"Maybe not." Bob chuckled.

"How long does it take?" Roger asked.

"The first directive? Oh, about five seconds," Bob said.

"That's it?" Roger asked.

"Yes," replied Bob.

"Okay, I have five seconds," said Roger.

"A burned-up brain won't start," Bob said in a flat voice.

"Pardon?" Roger asked.

"That's it. I worked all week trying to remember what Alice used to tell me. And this is the first thing I learned from her. She used to say that a burned-up brain just won't start," Bob said.

"So what can you do about it?" Roger asked, intrigued.

"Directive One—Recharge versus discharge," Bob said, looking at his little orange notebook.

Roger sat down and sipped his tea.

"All right, Bob, you have my attention. Tell me more," Roger said.

"What about your letter?" Bob asked.

"It can wait," Roger said, settling in his chair.

"Let me tell you, my Alice would have been happy to hear that you think her directive is worth listening to." Bob chuckled again. "Let's see, where was I?"

Bob checked his orange notebook.

"Oh, yes," Bob continued, "back in the years when Alice and I first got married, when you probably were toddling around on your tricycle, I used to work long hours and get home exhausted. Not unlike yourself. Until one night, Alice was waiting for me with a toolbox and a bunch of pine slats. That's how it started. She said she wanted a birdhouse, and she showed me a picture from a magazine. This was no ordinary birdhouse, but a fully decorated little bird cottage. Quite pretty, in fact."

"Were you a carpenter?"

"Me? No!" Bob curled up in laughter. "I was a businessman, like you, with a summa cum laude degree and lots of certificates, and I had never held a hammer in my life! But that didn't matter to Alice. She just wanted a birdhouse!"

"Did you build it?" Roger asked.

"Of course. There was no way to say no to Alice. I started

working on it the next evening. I was quite annoyed with her because I was so tired, but I cut some pieces and put them to one side. I also made a rough drawing and told Alice to get some more supplies that I would need the next day. I worked on that birdhouse for one whole week, every evening after work, until I finished it. It was only when I put the last bit of paint on it that I realized the truth about the birdhouse."

"What? That it was very ugly?" Roger joked.

"It wasn't the prettiest thing you've ever seen. But the truth is that the birdhouse was not for Alice." Bob shook his head, smiling.

"Who was it for?" Roger asked.

"It was for me," Bob replied.

"Sorry, Bob, I don't understand," Roger confessed.

"You see, the truth is that after the first evening, I wasn't annoyed any longer. I actually started to enjoy the work. In the morning, the first thing I did, even before reading the paper, was to go look at the birdhouse. About the third or fourth night I started singing while I was working. Do you see what I mean?"

"Maybe," Roger said tentatively.

"Alice had tried to show me that after discharging my energy at work all day, I needed to do something to recharge myself. Some people call it creative time, others call it leisure, but the truth is that what is fun for one person feels like work to another. You have to find something that is suitable for you. When I was sanding the wood and painting the birdhouse, I noticed that new thoughts just popped into my head. Things I had been struggling with for days seemed much clearer. I had ideas, and it was very exciting. If you keep pouring energy out and you don't recharge, then one day you'll run empty. You'll burn out."

"I know the feeling," admitted Roger.

"Exactly. I can recognize it because I've been through it myself," said Bob.

"So you just kept on building birdhouses?"

"Oh, no!" Bob guffawed. "That was the end of my brilliant career as a carpenter. That birdhouse ended up in the charity shop because no bird would ever come near it. But I did learn to recharge."

"What did you do?" Roger was concentrating and forgetting to drink his tea.

"Roger, don't let your tea get cold," said Bob. "Don't try to memorize this. It will come to you naturally."

Roger sipped his tea and unbuttoned his collar.

"I told Alice that I understood why she had asked me to build her birdhouse. She said she was relieved because that meant she wouldn't have to ask me to build another one. I thanked her for her insight, and she just said simply that a burned-up brain won't start. She said that I wouldn't expect my car to start if I let it run out of gas, so why would I expect my body to do so? Her wisdom was so straightforward that there really was no argument. So I found a way to recharge every day after work and sometimes even during work. I would go for a walk or read a nourishing book or magazine articles that filled me with life. It became a routine, just like eating or getting dressed. Every evening, after dinner and family time, I would take time for recharging," Bob concluded.

"It's not that simple." Roger sighed.

"I think that if you try it, you may be surprised at how easy it is," Bob stated.

"But I am not married to your Alice," Roger said, "and my family doesn't understand the pressures I am under."

"What makes you think they don't understand?" Bob asked.

"My wife, Darlene, keeps complaining every day that I don't spend enough time with her and our two little girls. The girls have all these expectations, and they want me to go to their school plays and softball games. I am just one man. I feel guilty all the time, but I can't be in a thousand places at the same time. Maybe family and work just don't mix."

"Maybe you are worrying too much," Bob said, "but if you give the directives a chance, I have a feeling that you will feel very different about your family and even your work."

"To tell you the truth, Bob, I am getting swallowed into

a deep black hole. I don't see how any of this can help me," Roger said.

"Just promise one thing," said Bob.

"What's that?" asked Roger.

"That you'll be here next Monday," Bob answered, getting up.

"Is it time to go?" Roger looked at his watch.

"See you next Monday. Same time?" Bob asked.

"You bet," Roger replied.

Without another word, Bob tore off a page from his orange notebook and handed it to Roger. He then slipped out of the break room to start his cleaning routine. Roger read the piece of paper: *Directive One—Recharge versus discharge.* Roger walked back to his office and got to work on his letter. Ten minutes later, he was surprised at how easy it had been to finish the e-mail that he had been fighting with all day.

CHAPTER**FOUR**

I t was dark when Roger got home, but the light was still on in the kitchen. There were two slices of pizza in a box on the kitchen counter, and the dishes from the girls' dinner were still in the sink. This was pizza night, the girls' favorite food in the entire world. Roger wanted to take a quick shower and then sit down to review a proposal that had to go out the following morning. He climbed the stairs in three strides and got to the girls' room where Darlene was sitting cross-legged on the carpet between the two beds, reading the girls a story.

"Daddy!" the two girls screamed, climbing up onto his neck.

Roger reached down and kissed Darlene on her forehead. She was smiling.

"Would you like to take over?" Darlene asked. "I could use the time to do the dishes while you finish the story."

"Yes, Daddy, please!" the girls echoed.

"Okay, but just for a few minutes and then off to sleep," he said obligingly.

Roger usually avoided story time. He felt silly reading children's books and making the funny voices. Darlene was a much better storyteller, and she wore a long, pointed silver hat with stars on it and tulle falling from the tip, like something a fairy godmother would have. Roger took off his jacket and shoes and slipped down onto the carpet while the two girls cuddled up under the covers.

"Don't forget the hat." Becca looked in the direction of the fairy godmother cone.

"Oh, I don't think so," protested Roger, and he started to read the story from the point where Darlene had left off.

Ten minutes later he could hear both girls breathing rhythmically, sound asleep. He slipped out quietly and joined Darlene in the kitchen.

"They are both asleep," Roger said. "They look so peaceful."

"They love it when you read their bedtime story." Darlene set down a plate for Roger. "That's all they'll talk about tomorrow at breakfast. It's such a treat for them." She had reheated the pizza and made a bowl of tossed salad.

"I like it too," Roger said as he sat down to eat. "Would you keep me company?"

Darlene hesitated.

"Are you sure? I just thought you wanted to be left alone like you usually do when you get home." She sat down on the edge of the kitchen counter, her long legs dangling like a girl on a swing. "How was work?"

"Torture. Let's talk about the girls," Roger grumbled.

"The usual. Sarah can't stop talking about her softball game, and Becca thinks that her invisible friend, Chuck, needs a haircut. Oh! And I bumped into Dr. Gordon at the store, so I asked him about Sarah's nightmares," Darlene reported.

"Oh, yes, I had almost forgotten about that," Roger said, tucking into his dinner.

Darlene's brow wrinkled.

"What did he say?" Roger asked between mouthfuls.

"He said it was normal for children to have nightmares; sometimes they even last for a few days in a row. He said some researchers think it is a way for children to work out their fears."

"What kind of fears?" Roger asked.

"I wish I knew. The other day Sarah mentioned that the parents of one of her schoolmates are getting a divorce, and she asked me if we were going to get a divorce too."

"What did you say?" Roger said, putting his fork down.

There was a heavy silence. Darlene sighed.

"I asked her what made her think that," Darlene finally said, "and Sarah said that she had heard me crying in my bedroom."

"Why didn't you tell her that we are not getting a divorce?" Roger asked.

"I don't know," Darlene replied.

"What do you mean, you don't know?" Roger shot back.

"She just caught me at a vulnerable moment." Darlene looked down. "I know I was supposed to reassure her . . . that was what she was asking for . . . but how am I supposed to be sure if I don't really understand all that is going on? The last thing I want to do is to hurt my girls, but I am not going to lie to them."

"Why *were* you crying in our bedroom?" Roger asked.

"If you really have to ask, then there is no point in telling you, is there?" Darlene's voice was tense.

"How can I guess if you don't tell me?" Roger pushed his half-eaten food away.

"I've told you a thousand times, including last night, and I just refuse to have an argument every day. You married me. Do you remember? I didn't force you into some kind of miserable fate that is out of your control. You seem to see this family as a yoke that has been imposed on you, as some kind of obligation or burden that has gotten too heavy for you. Almost like something that happened to you while you weren't looking. All along I thought this was what we wanted. What *you* wanted. We were so happy when the girls arrived; life was so full, so magical. When we just got married, you couldn't wait to get back home. Now I almost feel like you would rather be single again, like you resent the family that we have built together. What good is the house, the cars, or the perfect vacation if you don't feel wanted or loved or needed? I just don't know anymore. You don't get it." Darlene slid down from the counter and trotted upstairs to the bedroom.

Roger wasn't hungry anymore. Yes, she had indeed told him a thousand times, and a thousand times Roger didn't understand her. He had provided a beautiful home and a stable situation for Darlene and the girls. He worked hard every day, mainly thinking about their well-being. So he didn't understand when Darlene spoke of the distance between them, the absence, or the detachment. Roger couldn't figure out how she could run hot and cold in what seemed like one instant. She had an idealized vision of what their life should be, filled with images of cozy dinners around the table and trips to the park and Little League games. But that's just not the way things had turned out in real life, and when reality didn't match her version of how life should be, she stormed off in a whirlwind of contempt.

Roger tossed his dishes in the dishwasher and looked for his briefcase. He'd have to read that proposal tonight or else there wouldn't be time to make any corrections tomorrow. There was no way that he could make Darlene understand how urgent these things were. He could not let his business obligations slide. He was the head of a company that employed dozens of workers, who had families to support. Roger rummaged for the proposal but could not find it.

I can't believe it. Did I leave the printout at the office?

For a second he considered calling Becky at home to see if she could e-mail him a copy, but it was too late for that. Driving to the office and back would take at least one hour. He might as well, once again, get to work at the crack of dawn. Roger prepared to get into bed and hopefully get some sleep. Darlene had already turned her reading light off, obviously not in the mood for any further socializing. He set the alarm for 5:30 and knelt down next to Darlene's night table shelves to look at a pile of books there. He hadn't noticed that Darlene was such a prolific reader. Roger picked up one book at random. It was a copy of *Living Beyond the Limits* by Franklin Graham.

Sounds like me, living beyond my limits.

Roger started reading without paying much attention, hoping to doze off without the need of a sleeping pill. Two hours later he was still wide-awake but deeply immersed in the stories of people surmounting incredible obstacles to serve the needs of others in faith. Roger read stories of selfless humanitarians working in wartime conditions in Angola and Beirut and so many other human situations where hope was not a word to be used lightly. The stories in Graham's book stirred something inside Roger. His thoughts traveled to the soldiers who were today fighting for his own freedom in foreign lands. Some of them would never come back home to their families; some fathers would never be there to read a bedtime story to their little children. Roger was not thinking of the business proposal anymore. He reset the alarm clock to 7:30 a.m. and kept reading until almost midnight when he finally slipped down into his pillow and fell asleep.

In the morning, Darlene nudged Roger's side as the alarm went off.

"Did you sleep in? It's 7:30!" Darlene said.

"That's fine. I needed some proper rest," Roger said, getting up. "Maybe I can drop off the girls at school."

"Really?" Darlene jumped up from bed.

"Would I get a smile if I do?" Roger stood in the doorway.

"You'd get a smile and blueberry pancakes with maple syrup!" Darlene grinned.

"Deal," said Roger.

Roger showered and got dressed while Darlene woke up the girls and started breakfast. It was a new feeling to be home during these preparations. Usually he would leave the house while everyone else was asleep, like a timid guest slipping away from a party. The girls were so lovely in the morning, with their sleepy faces bent over their cereal bowls.

"I started reading one of your books last night, the one by Franklin Graham," Roger said while he enjoyed his breakfast.

"*Living Beyond the Limits*? Isn't it fascinating?" Darlene gave no sign of harboring any resentment from last night. It was one of her many positive qualities, recovering from an argument into a completely fresh start.

"Amazing. I couldn't stop reading. Those people are something special," Roger said. "I could never do something like that."

"I think you could. You are always helping people and reaching out to others," Darlene said.

That is the nicest thing Darlene has said to me in a long time, Roger thought.

"Are you sure about driving the girls?" Darlene whispered, glancing in their direction.

Roger nodded. He ate his breakfast and helped get the girls ready for school and into the car. Before he drove off, he looked back at Darlene. There was his wife, still in her pajamas, hair in a tussle, and smiling. She looked just like a grown-up version of Becca. She waved good-bye and mouthed, "Thank-you." In broad daylight, it now seemed unreal that last night they had mentioned divorce; it now seemed so natural to be a unit. Darlene, Becca, and Sarah—they were Roger's world. How could things get so complicated that by this very evening he might be going over the same argument with Darlene all over again? How could this calm and sparkling sea turn into a tempest all of a sudden?

On the way to school, the girls brought Roger up to date on Sarah's softball exploits and Chuck's desperate need for an invisible haircut. Roger was enjoying the crisp, shiny morning.

As soon as he got to work, Roger asked Becky to hold his calls until he finished reading the proposal. Sitting down at his desk, he saw the crinkled page from Bob's little notebook. *Directive One—Recharge versus discharge.* Roger realized that reading the inspiring book last night had filled him with energy this morning. Even connecting with Darlene in conversation at breakfast had been effortless.

So this recharging is not so hard after all. Maybe Bob has a point.

Roger read the proposal in thirty minutes without interruptions and handed over his comments to Becky with plenty of time to make the corrections and submit it before the deadline. Roger could not understand why this task had seemed so impossible yesterday. Then he remembered.

A burned-up brain won't start.

CHAPTER FIVE

The next Monday Roger was in the break room before Bob arrived.

"Hi, there!" Bob greeted him with a hint of surprise. "You beat me to the tea-making duties today."

"I am a changed man," Roger announced, setting the mugs down.

Roger told Bob about his breakfast with his daughters and how much he had enjoyed taking them to school. He also related how much easier it had been to work when he was well rested.

"I read a most amazing book," Roger said, "*Living Beyond the Limits* by Franklin Graham. Have you read it?"

"No, I haven't. I've heard about it, though."

"You can borrow it," offered Roger. "I'll bring it next week."

"Thank-you, but don't trouble yourself. You are such a busy man," Bob said.

"No trouble. Besides, I have learned to recharge versus

discharge, so I won't let work overwhelm me any longer." Roger nodded firmly.

"I'm really glad it's working out for you," said Bob, looking at his tea.

"I'll apologize if I am misreading the situation, but you don't seem excited for me. Is there something wrong?" Roger said with a somewhat puzzled expression.

"Not at all. I am very happy for you. It's just that . . ." Bob stopped.

"Go ahead, you can tell me," Roger said.

"Well, I wouldn't wish you to be disappointed. You are certainly off to a good start, but the changes that the directives set off in your life are for the long term. We live in a culture of instant, ready-made results. But life doesn't always work that way. Sometimes things seem to get worse before they get better."

"Meaning?" Roger asked.

"What I am trying to say, very ineffectively, is that you should not get too focused on short-term reactions or on 'making it work.' Because if you do, and any little thing goes wrong, you'll blame the directives or me or the weather, instead of realizing that there will always be things going wrong. The directives work at a deep level, below the surface of anecdotal events." Bob looked up at Roger as he finished saying this.

A thick silence followed.

"But do you want to know what I find extremely exciting?" asked Bob finally.

"What's that?" Roger replied.

"The fact that you kept your promise. You are here. That is all I asked, and you kept your word," said Bob with a broad smile.

Roger smiled back.

"Look what I got today," Roger said, whipping out a little orange notebook, identical to the one Bob always carried with him.

Bob had to chuckle.

"I'm ready for you, Bob. Let me have Directive Two," said Roger.

"Okay, here we go. Let's see," said Bob, checking his notebook. "Here it is."

Bob paused a moment, as if to decide where to begin.

"After Alice showed me how to balance work and rest," Bob commenced, "I became very productive. It was funny, because although it required less effort from me, I actually was doing better work. Our first child had arrived, so we were really busy at home, but Alice coped with graceful ease. She enjoyed being a mother. I was feeling really proud and important. I was a family man now."

"I know exactly what you mean. The day our Sarah arrived, I felt I could walk on water." Roger nodded.

"Exactly," said Bob, "and then the first colic arrives and sleepless nights with a crying baby that you just don't know how to soothe. It can be distressing. But as I said, my Alice was a natural. She never seemed frazzled. Those were happy days. We would spend the entire evening stretched out on the carpet, just looking at our beautiful baby and laughing at her little noises. Anyway, I went off on a tangent. It usually happens when I talk about my children." Bob chuckled. "About the same time, my bosses noticed my improved productivity. I was acing one contract after another; I could do no wrong. So they offered me a promotion."

"That's great!" said Roger.

"Indeed, I was very gratified. It meant more responsibility and the opportunity to earn a share of the profits as opposed to a fixed income."

"Sounds like a winner," Roger said.

"It was. But it can be tricky as well. You see, just before our baby arrived, we had decided that it was time to own our first home. So we moved out of our rented apartment into a lovely little house and took out a mortgage. It was going to be tight, but we would keep a close eye on the budget, and with my salary we could make it. Then the promotion came and with it the opportunity to earn more money. But the problem was that I didn't have a fixed salary anymore, and I started to worry about paying the mortgage and meeting all the expenses that come with a new family."

"I see what you mean." Roger nodded.

"Everything indicated that I would enjoy a comfortable income in my new position, particularly taking into consideration my stellar performance up to then, but all the obligations I had at home just made it feel like the promotion was the right thing at the wrong time. I don't want to sound ungrateful, but that was how I felt at the time."

"Yeah, and lack of sleep doesn't help to think straight, right?" Roger said.

"Talk about lack of sleep. Our baby was only six months old when Alice found out that the second was on the way!" Bob shook his head. "In three years I went from being a carefree single to father of three!"

"You didn't waste any time, did you?" Roger teased.

"I told you, Alice loved being a mother. Anyway, the production stopped at three, and it is great to see that our three children are best friends; being so close in age, they have lots in common. But it was an interesting time, I tell you."

"So how did the new job go?" Roger asked.

"Very well. I learned the ropes quickly and put all my energy behind my production goals. I exceeded the targets and earned a substantial bonus," Bob said flatly, "but I started to resent my boss. I thought he had unreasonable expectations for me."

"Did he?" Roger asked.

"Not really," Bob acknowledged. "All my targets were set by mutual agreement and reviewed monthly for any adjustments. I was pretty much setting my own speed. Except I didn't know where to stop. I kept stretching myself until I snapped."

"You? I can't believe it." Roger arched his eyebrows.

"Oh, yeah," admitted Bob, "and on Thanksgiving, of all days. We were having dinner at Alice's parents' home. Alice and her mother had prepared the most wonderful meal with the perfect turkey and all the traditional trimmings. Everybody was having a great time. I remember Alice's sister and her husband had announced that they were expecting their first baby. It was one of those perfect family snapshots. Then one of our children accidentally knocked over a glass of grape juice. It went all over the white embroidered tablecloth. Not exactly a catastrophe, I know, but I just saw red. I got up from the table, removed the child from his high chair, and told Alice, point-blank in front of her entire family, that if she couldn't control 'her children,' she shouldn't have had so many."

"Wow!" whispered Roger.

"Wow is right. What a thing to say. Everyone went quiet,

and Alice turned pale. For some reason, seeing her upset made me behave even more irrationally. I launched into the most bitter tirade. I ranted without taking a breath, spewing venom at her and the children about the pressure that was imposed on me to cope with the demands of my career. I am too embarrassed to repeat what I said. It was awful. Alice did not say a word. She gathered the children, and we went home in complete silence."

"Was she mad at you?" asked Roger.

"Oh, I'm sure she wasn't exactly pleased, but she never said a hurtful word to me in her entire life. She did get her revenge, though."

"What did she do?"

"She embroidered my favorite bowling shirt," Bob said solemnly.

"I'm sorry?" Roger asked, muffling a laugh.

"Every Friday at lunchtime I went bowling with my boss and two of my colleagues. It was a staff meeting of sorts. We discussed the week and planned for the next. Alice always packed my bowling ball and clothes in a sports bag. The Friday after my Thanksgiving episode, I pulled out my bowling shirt to find it had words embroidered on the front and back. I didn't have a choice but to put it on, having nothing else to wear, as was Alice's intention, of course. I guess I deserved it."

"What did the shirt say?"

"It contained the second of Alice's directives. I bowled three games with my boss and coworkers while wearing a shirt that read: 'My family is a blessing, not a responsibility.'"

Roger stared at Bob a moment and then burst out laughing. His eyes were watering.

Directive 2: View family as a blessing, not a responsibility.

"You don't have to laugh so hard, you know." Bob chuckled along.

"I'm sorry." Roger paused for breath. "It's just so perfect!"

"Indeed, as you can well imagine, everyone wanted to know why I was wearing this particular legend on my shirt." Bob sighed. "So I had to tell about my momentary lapse of reason at the Thanksgiving table and Alice's way of sending me a message," Bob said. "The funny thing is, every single one of my bowling buddies could relate. They had been feeling the same pressure and resented their families for the demands that were placed on them. Maybe it was a product of my generation, but we all saw our families as a responsibility, the reason we must work, to put food on the table and a roof over their heads."

"I think it still applies today," Roger said.

"This mind-set lends itself to several problems. It becomes hard to enjoy work because work becomes a necessary evil to meet the burden of responsibility at home. If the purpose of work is defined as providing for home life, then it becomes hard to enjoy either work or home. So when work is miserable, naturally it is home's fault. By the time we finished the last frame, we all agreed that Alice had a point and that we had been looking at it the wrong way around."

"So how should you look at it then?" Roger leaned forward in his chair.

"Very simple. If you view your family as a blessing, not a responsibility, you can experience joy with your family. Then you are able to experience your work in a fresh and free way— free from viewing it as slave work to provide for home—you become free to uncover your real purpose for work."

"And what is that?" Roger asked.

"That is a question you must ask yourself," Bob said as he put the notebook back in his shirt pocket, "because your purpose may be different from mine. Now that we have established that owning Triple A is not merely for the purpose of putting food on the table, ask yourself, 'What is my true purpose here?'"

"I don't know," Roger responded.

"You know," Bob said. "You have just temporarily forgotten. Take your time to think about it. Once you uncover that purpose, you will become excited about your work, and work will become fun again. It will have meaning. For people who truly understand and live out their purpose, work does not seem like work."

"Did you find your purpose?" Roger asked.

"It took me a while, but I did."

"What was it?" Roger asked.

"I'll tell you after you've found yours. I don't want to confuse your search. Let's just say that I am still fulfilling it today, this very instant, talking to you." Bob got up to start his cleaning rounds. "I'll see you next Monday then. Thanks for the tea."

"You bet," said Roger.

"Oh, one more thing," Bob said over his shoulder. "After I found my purpose, I was able to come home satisfied with my work. That made it easier to relax and enjoy my family. I am so grateful for that. Now that Alice is gone, I realize that all our experiences were so precious. Alice was right. My family was my biggest blessing, and still is today."

After Bob left, Roger wrote the directive in his own little notebook: *Directive Two: View family as a blessing, not a responsibility.* He went back to his office to find that his wife and two daughters were waiting for him there. His heart tightened.

CHAPTER SIX

A s Roger walked toward his office, Sarah and Becca ran
to him and hugged his knees. Roger leaned down to
kiss them and looked up to his wife.

"Is everything okay?" he asked.

"Yes. Why?" Darlene replied.

"Nothing. It's just that you rarely come to the office. I
thought something was wrong."

"I'm sorry we startled you," said Darlene. "Your mobile
was turned off, and the girls wanted to invite you to a gourmet dinner to celebrate. Sarah was picked to be the pitcher
in the next softball game."

"Really!" Roger tickled Sarah between her ribs. "Do we
have a champion in the family?"

"Daddy, stop!" Sarah giggled.

"So can you come, Daddy?" Becca chimed in. "Pleeeeeze?"

"Well . . ." Roger paused for a second, thinking of the
mountain of e-mails he had not even read today. "Absolutely.
Wouldn't miss it for the world."

Amid cheers and leaps of excitement, the Kimbrough family made it to the car.

"Where to, fair ladies?" asked Roger.

"Oh, I should have warned you," Darlene said with a smile. "It's a gourmet dinner Sarah's style, so naturally the menu is . . ."

"Pizza, pizza, pizza!" sang the two girls from the backseat.

"But they promised to eat their salads as well without a peep," said Darlene.

"That's right," said Roger. "An athlete can't live on pizza alone!"

They arrived at the cheerful Italian restaurant and settled at their table, covered in a crisp red-and-white-checked tablecloth and adorned with a posy of fresh flowers. Becca pulled up an empty chair right next to her own. The server brought two coloring books and crayons for the girls and offered to remove the empty chair to make more space.

"No!" said Becca. "It's for Chuck."

Puzzled, the server looked at Darlene.

"Imaginary friend," Darlene explained.

"Of course." He winked at Becca. "Would Chuck like a coloring book too?"

"I'll ask him," said Becca, leaning over. "Chuck says he is too old to play with crayons, but he says thank-you anyway."

"I'll be back with your beverage order in a minute." The server smiled and left.

Darlene looked at Roger and shrugged. Both assumed that Becca's imaginary friend was a little boy about her own age or younger.

He whispered to Darlene, "So how old is this Chuck really supposed to be?"

"I don't know," she whispered back.

"Shouldn't we ask Becca?"

"Maybe . . ." Darlene said under her breath, "but maybe it is better not to make a fuss about it."

The whole business of Chuck made Darlene uneasy, so Roger changed the subject, thinking that he should have been paying more attention. He made a mental note to track this Chuck character more closely.

"So when is your big game then, Sarah?"

"Thursday afternoon," Sarah replied in a timid voice. "Can you . . ."

"Sarah," Darlene intercepted gently, "you know Daddy is busy at work."

"Can't promise, but I'll try to make it," Roger said.

Sarah and Becca gave Roger a huge smile. Darlene gave him one of her looks.

"What?" he whispered while the girls were drawing with their crayons.

"Roger," Darlene said, "you know."

Roger raised his eyebrows.

"I don't want Sarah to be disappointed if you don't show up," Darlene whispered back. "You know how hard she took it last time you forgot."

"Don't worry," Roger said, placing his hand gently over his wife's slender fingers. "I won't forget again."

Darlene looked up at Roger but didn't remove her hand from under his. Roger pressed her hand and looked into her eyes.

"I won't forget," he repeated.

The food arrived, and the server placed the salad bowls next to each plate and left the bubbling pizza pie in the center of the table.

Darlene looked down at Roger's hand, still holding hers.

"I will need my hand to serve the pizza," she said, smiling softly.

"I'm afraid we will have to find an alternative solution," Roger said, "because I am not releasing this hand at the moment."

The two girls giggled, and Roger saw Darlene's cheeks turn a deeper shade of pink.

"Girls," Roger said, "can you think of a possible solution?"

"I know," Sarah said. "I'll serve!"

"That's a great idea," Roger affirmed.

Sarah knelt on her chair and stretched her little arms as far as they would go. She carefully scooped each slice of pizza and handed the plates back without dropping a single speck. Becca fell into fits of giggles.

"But, Daddy," Becca said, "now you'll have to let go because Mommy has to eat."

"Okay," Roger agreed, "but only while she eats; then she has to give it back."

The girls were enjoying the game and started to eat their salads without having to be reminded. For the first time in years, Roger felt at ease being exactly where he wanted to be without the nagging thought that he was supposed to be somewhere else. He didn't even feel guilty nor did Darlene resist when he decided to head back to the office to do a few more things that evening. Darlene drove the two girls home and tucked them into bed, exhausted and contented.

• • •

Thursday afternoon, however, found Roger entangled in an unforeseen complication. His assistant, Becky, had four unexpected visitors waiting for him in the lobby.

"These gentlemen are here on behalf of Crockett Steel," Becky said with a tight smile and handed Roger the four business cards that the visitors had presented.

Roger looked at the cards, all bearing the logo of the same company, a quality-management firm.

"We are here for the quality audit, Mr. Kimbrough," said one of the four men, shaking Roger's hand.

"I'm sorry?" said Roger.

He looked over at Becky. Could it be that he had forgotten about this appointment? But Becky shrugged her shoulders and shook her head slightly. Roger paused a moment.

"There must be a mistake," Roger said. "I don't think we were scheduled for an audit."

"No, we were sent by Crockett Steel," said the consultant. "I have the paperwork here if you'd like to . . ."

"Becky," Roger interrupted, "can you get me the CEO of Crockett Steel on the phone please?"

The consultant took out a clipboard from his briefcase and cleared his throat.

"It shouldn't take more than a couple of hours, Mr. Kimbrough," he said, fidgeting with his tie. "I assumed you knew we were coming."

"No, I didn't know you were coming," stated Roger, "and it is really not a good time. We are extremely busy at the moment."

"I appreciate that, sir," the consultant replied, "but we are just following the instructions from our client."

Becky finally got the phone call through to the CEO of Crockett Steel and transferred it to Roger.

"It's not a big deal, Roger," said Barton Woods amid loud static. "Just a bunch of forms to fill in and you're done."

"I know, Barton, but you could have given me at least a twenty-four-hour notice," Roger replied. "We can do the audit on Monday, but today is just not a good time."

"Whatever you say, Roger. It's just that our quality-management people need all our suppliers to be aligned with our efforts. You know we are pushing hard for this ISO certification. Our Eastern Europe clients are joining the European Union, blah, blah, the regulations and all that hoopla, and they've given us an ultimatum. We need to get certified pronto. You know the story. I thought you were on board too."

"Of course, I am," Roger replied. "You know we're already ISO certified. It's just that I don't have extra people to pull out to show these guys around today."

There was a loud sound of static again.

"You're breaking up, Barton," said Roger.

"I know, I'm at the airport. Look, Roger, can we be practical and let these guys do their thing? Let's not make it more complicated," Woods asked.

"Barton, the . . ." Roger stopped as the line was disconnected.

Roger looked at his watch. He could see the consultants milling around outside his door, waiting. Then he remembered Sarah's softball game and Darlene's prophetic words:

I don't want her to be disappointed. She took it so hard last time you forgot.

How could he explain to Darlene that his day had spun out of control? It clearly wasn't his fault. He hadn't made the auditors appear; he couldn't have planned it at a worse time if he had intended to. At the same time, Roger realized that if any of this was to change, it was now up to him.

• • •

"Big hit, Sarah! You can do it!" Roger yelled excitedly as his seven-year-old stepped up to the plate with the score tied at seven.

Sarah smiled back and then proceeded to slap the ball just over the shortstop's head to drive home the winning run. After the game, Sarah—flush with excitement—ran over to hug her elated dad.

"Did you see that? Did you see that hit I made, Daddy?" she asked.

"That was fantastic." Roger hugged her tight. "Did you have fun?"

Sarah nodded heartily and skipped ahead, unable to keep still.

The coach patted Roger on the back.

"Good you could make it, Mr. Kimbrough," he said.

"She's been telling everyone that her dad's coming to the game."

"The team did a good job." Roger nodded in the direction of a group of little players.

"They are something, aren't they? And your Sarah is some ballplayer. She never gives up. She got turned down for the team twice, but she kept practicing until she made pitcher. I wish I had her determination."

Roger wondered why Sarah had never mentioned the times she had been turned down. It seemed such an adult thing to do to keep her disappointment to herself. Maybe she didn't think he would understand.

Where have I been? Who have I been?

Roger walked back to the car, holding Darlene's hand, watching his two girls skipping and playing along. He was beginning to understand the meaning in Bob's words. His family was truly a blessing, and he had been feeling that it was a burden. He would no longer make that mistake. But as soon as he checked his voice mail, the spell was broken. Five of the messages were from Fred Hopper, his longtime CFO. Roger had literally dumped the quality consultants on Fred to finish the audit so that he could make little Sarah's game. The audit was obviously giving Fred a headache, or he would not have called so many times.

I should have rescheduled that wretched audit.

Roger drove back to the office with a feeling of foreboding. The theory of the directives was all very well, but in practice, how could someone with his responsibility possibly focus on family with all the problems he had at work? Today he had just sneaked out for two hours, and the office was already on fire. Could someone like Janitor Bob possibly understand the depth of his issues at work?

CHAPTER SEVEN

Bob looked at his watch again and tapped his fingers on his mug. Roger was running late this Monday. It was not a surprise to Bob. In fact, he was curious to see if Roger would show up at all. Then, about fifteen minutes later, the door to the break room swung wide open.

"Roger!" Bob said. "It's good to see you."

"Sorry for being late," Roger stated, "but I said I'd be here, and here I am."

They settled down with fresh mugs of tea, and Bob got straight to the point.

"Having trouble?" Bob asked.

"I'm afraid so. But it has nothing to do with you. Don't worry," Roger said. "I still appreciate your kindness. I'm sure your directives are great—they are just not for me."

"What gave you that impression?"

"Well, you know, I'm in too deep. It's just too difficult to turn it around now. This week I couldn't even recharge through my little girl's ball game without having a major fire at work. My family is a blessing and not a burden, but every time I try to improve one side of the equation, the other side gets even worse."

Roger described how the surprise audit by the major client had disrupted an extremely busy day and how the events had deteriorated until half his staff was trying to reach him on his cell phone. Bob listened attentively, nodding his head every now and then.

"I'm stuck," Roger concluded. "I'll end up in divorce at home or bankruptcy at work."

"Or both!" Bob added.

Roger looked up in surprise.

"It could get even worse, let me tell you," Bob declared, looking up at the ceiling. "Just when I was learning to view my family as a blessing and not a burden, things got really good at work too. I was handling a huge, exclusive deal to manufacture this breakthrough medical device invented by a German scientist. It would take up our whole production capacity for at least the next five years with an enormous potential for expansion internationally. We had all the certifications lined up, and we were sure we had the best bid. All I had to do was submit our response to the German developer's Request for Proposals, and it would be a silk road after that. At the same time, life at home was bliss."

"Too good to be true?" Roger said.

"Correct. The week of the RFP I ended up in the hospital. I had a rough couple of days, and after some testing, I was diagnosed with diabetes," Bob recalled.

"I'm so sorry. I had no idea," Roger said with feeling.

"So the RFP was dead in the water. I didn't make the deadline. This great opportunity dissolved right between my fingers. I let my entire company down. So naturally I spent hour upon hour in the hospital, moping about my fate."

"Let me guess. Alice did not approve of moping," Roger said with a chuckle.

"You bet." Bob laughed. "She was ready for me. I got this beautiful bunch of flowers and balloons delivered to my room with a simple note on a card."

"Directive Three?" Roger asked.

"You guessed it," replied Bob. "Do you mind if I ask you a very personal question?"

"Go ahead, I'm ready." Roger smiled, putting up his fists like a boxer.

"Are you a man of faith?" Bob asked.

Roger paused a moment.

"You don't have to answer that if . . ." Bob said, shaking his head slowly.

"No," said Roger, "I don't mind. I am a Christian. I even remember when I became one."

"You do?" Bob smiled.

"Vividly. I was twelve. Summer camp. There was a group of kids teasing this girl. She was tall and had very skinny legs, and they were all giving her a hard time, calling her *Matchsticks* and other worse names. But then there was this other group of four kids, two brothers and two sisters, who broke up the crowd and were really friendly with the girl and included her in their group. I was impressed by their kindness and told them so. They said it was the way of their Christian faith, and they told me more about their church and their relationship with Christ. At the time it made a lot of sense to me, and I wanted to have that type of relationship with God. They told me how I could trust Christ as my personal Savior. That day, I prayed and asked Jesus into my heart even though I have not done very well living out my faith. And you know what else?"

"The skinny girl?" Bob winked.

"She turned out to be a late bloomer and became prom queen. Who would have known?"

"Do you know what became of her?" Bob asked.

"She's my wife, Darlene!" Roger's face lit up.

"That's a beautiful love story!" Bob chuckled.

"It was," Roger almost whispered.

"Still is," Bob asserted.

Roger paused before he made a comment. "Yes, I suppose it still is. But I don't know for how much longer."

Both men sipped their tea in silence.

"But you were telling me about your diabetes. How is that going?" Roger asked.

"Oh, no big deal," Bob said with a dismissive wave of his hand. "I was blessed. I had good doctors, and my wife was very supportive, so I followed their directions, adjusted my lifestyle, and got it under control. And not only did I follow the doctors' directions, but I followed Alice's directive."

Directive 3: Pray; don't pout.

"What did it say?" asked Roger.

"Well, the message on the card said simply: Pray; don't pout."

Roger let out a high-pitched laugh. "I'm sorry," Roger said, drawing his breath. "I'm not laughing at you. I'm laughing at myself. I suddenly realized that all I've done today is pout."

"So you still think Alice's directives are not for you?" Now it was Bob's turn to laugh.

"Alice had a way of hitting the nail on the head, didn't she?" Roger replied, reaching for his little orange notebook.

"You got it," Bob said.

"So what happened at work then?" Roger asked.

"Nobody was really happy about losing the deal, of course, but the concern about my health put everything else in the background. Mainly, everyone was relieved that my health was improving. Then a few months later we heard that the competitor who had won the RFP had sunk a few hundred thousand into development before being hit by a lawsuit that froze the whole deal. As it turns out, there was a dispute over the patent rights, and it became so convoluted that it got caught up in court for good. That company was never able to recover its investment."

"So it turned out to be a good thing to lose the RFP?" Roger asked.

"Exactly. But I didn't know it at the time, of course, and I thought that losing the RFP was a catastrophe. So you never know. Sometimes it is better to take a step backward in order to better march forward."

"I really appreciate your telling me these stories, Bob," Roger said.

"It is my privilege, Roger. If any of my experience can help you, that fulfills my purpose in this world. I learned so much from Alice that I vowed to share her directives with any-one who may be able to benefit from her wisdom," said Bob, tapping his little orange notebook.

"I am certainly benefiting," Roger acknowledged, tapping his own little orange notebook.

"Maybe one day you can do the same for someone else," Bob said.

A cloud passed over Roger's face.

"Bob, do you think I'm pouting?"

"No, I didn't mean to say you were pouting." Bob smiled. "I'm just sharing Alice's directive, and you can apply it to the situation as it fits. It may not be as personal for you as it was for me."

"Even if I wanted to pray," Roger said almost to himself, "I don't know that I would remember what to do. It's been so long. What would I pray about?"

"That's the beauty of prayer," Bob said. "God already knows your situation. He even knows what tomorrow holds. He is just waiting for you to open up and let Him help you. You could start by telling God that you are sorry for turning away from Him all these years."

"Makes sense," Roger said.

"If you are up for it, there's more."

"Go ahead." Roger nodded.

"Then you could also ask Him to refresh you with His Spirit and to begin to give you clear insight into the challenges that you are having at Triple A and also at home. Then a good way to get to the next step is to ask God for *favor* and *wisdom*."

"What do you mean by that?" Roger asked.

"It's really quite simple," Bob replied. "Ask God to grant you favor to understand the problems of Triple A and wisdom so that you can handle them effectively. The same holds true for trouble at home. You can't really do anything about it if you don't understand the root of the problem. If you react without understanding, you are merely bumping blindly into one unresolved obstacle after another. So it is common sense to pray for favor so that you will understand, and then, of course, you need wisdom to know what kind of action to take. In your case you could also ask for favor that your wife, Darlene, will be able to put the past in the past and give you the chance to be the husband and father that God meant you to be."

Roger looked down and studiously smoothed the crease of his pants.

"Does this kind of talk make you uncomfortable?" Bob asked. "I didn't mean to impose my beliefs on you."

"Absolutely not." Roger shook his head.

In his private thoughts, however, Roger had felt a slight touch of awkwardness. Was Bob getting a little too spiritual on him? If he reached deep down, Roger would have to admit that he had dropped the ball on God. It was one of the bones of contention with Darlene. She had often requested that they go to church more often as a family and teach the girls to pray. Roger had always been too busy. Darlene would go by herself and take the girls, but she would never talk about it because she could sense Roger's lack of interest. However he looked at it, Roger could hardly find a good reason why he shouldn't give prayer a chance. Except that he was still so busy.

"One last thing," Bob said. "Sometimes when your plate is full, God will give you great insight on what is important to focus on and what needs to be removed from your plate entirely."

Roger looked up. Was Bob reading his mind?

"When you have to choose," Bob continued, "it is nice to be able to separate the significant relationships and responsibilities in your life from the junk that seems urgent but has no meaningful reason to be on the plate. It starts with praying. If you are up for it, just turn it over to God and see what happens."

Roger started shaking his head slowly from side to side.

"I'm not very persuasive, am I?" Bob said.

"No," Roger said, "it's not that. Quite the contrary."

Roger paused to reflect. When he spoke again, his voice had a new softness.

"I've just realized that I've been a selfish blockhead," Roger admitted.

"Why?" Bob asked.

"It's my new neighbor," Roger replied. "He's been asking me over for a cup of coffee for weeks now, and I never find the time. I just realized that he may be looking for my support; he told me he started a new business. I've basically ignored the guy."

"Don't be too hard on yourself. You had your own troubles," Bob said. "Besides, you can still accept his invitation and go over for coffee."

Roger brightened up. "Yes, I'll make a point of it. Maybe I'll share Alice's directives with him."

"There you go. We can start a franchise." Bob laughed.

"From now on, I won't pout," Roger said.

"Remember that the directive also says, *Pray*."

"I'm afraid I haven't prayed in such a long time, Bob," said Roger.

"We can kick-start your new praying career immediately. We can practice right now if you don't mind," Bob said, folding his hands around his booklet.

"All right," Roger agreed.

Bob paused a moment and then said in a very gentle voice, "Dear Lord, we thank You for this time together and for blessing us with our families and friends. Please grant Roger Your favor and wisdom on the road to rebuild a peaceful and joyful home and find prosperity in his work, and guide him to help his neighbor in need. In the name of Jesus Christ, our Lord, amen."

"Amen," whispered Roger.

"That didn't hurt, did it?" Bob asked.

"It felt really good," Roger admitted.

"It is just like having an ongoing conversation with your

best friend," observed Bob. "God is always ready to listen. Like I said. Just turn it over to God and see what happens."

Bob got up and was all business again, picking up the two mugs so that he could wash them.

"I'll see you next Monday then?" Roger asked.

"You bet," Bob replied.

As Roger closed the door behind him, he heard Bob break out into one of his operas. Roger recognized this one; it was Verdi's *Il Trovatore*.

"Miserere d'un'alma già vicina alla partenza": have mercy upon a soul who is about to embark on a journey.

CHAPTER**EIGHT**

Roger returned to his office after talking to Bob and found his CFO, Fred Hopper, waiting for him. Fred was a close friend as well as the one person who had been with Roger through thick and thin ever since the beginning of Triple A.

"You're still here, Fred?" Roger asked.

"We have a situation," Fred said.

"Let me guess. Crockett Steel?" Roger sighed.

"I just received an e-mail from the company's purchasing manager saying that we need to cut prices across the board by 12 percent if we want to continue to do business with Crockett. Did you know anything about this?"

"Not a thing," Roger said, picking up a paper clip. "I spoke with the CEO the day of the audit, and you would think he'd mention this little detail. Did he say why?"

"Not in the e-mail. But I called up the purchasing guy, and off the record, apparently JKM Metalworks has provided Crockett with a proposal to undercut us. Since JKM

Metalworks is a roll-up of many small companies, my guess is that it is going for market share to bump up gross sales volume in a push to take the company public. JKM certainly couldn't be in business to make a profit if this is the way it is pricing."

"There is no way we can cut our prices again," Roger said, twisting and bending one paper clip after another.

"I know," replied Fred, "but we can't afford to lose our largest customer. Are you going to call an emergency management-team meeting?"

"We always seem to be in an emergency lately." Roger kept torturing the paper clips.

In the past, the emergency meetings would have started at whatever time the emergency presented itself, even late into the night, and would have continued uninterrupted until a solution or recommendation was agreed upon. Every single member of the team dreaded these meetings because they always caused resentment with their families.

"Not our fault really. It's these guys at Crockett Steel who keep squeezing us," Fred said, expecting Roger to call the meeting.

"Let me pray about this," Roger said.

Fred did a double take. "Pardon?"

"I think I could use some special guidance," Roger stated.

"Did you just say *pray*?" Fred asked.

"Trust me on this one. I'll explain later. For now, call a meeting of the management team for 1:00 p.m. tomorrow, and then go home and recharge. We will discuss the letter tomorrow. In the meantime, don't tell anyone else about it."

"Recharge?" Fred squinted at Roger as if looking at him for the first time.

"Yes, recharge. Do something you enjoy. Play with the kids, read a book, whatever you do to unwind."

"I play golf," said Fred.

"Well, you can't play golf this late. There's got to be something else," said Roger.

"I . . ." Fred started.

"What?" Roger asked.

"Nothing, forget it," Fred mumbled.

"Come on, Fred. We're friends." Roger smiled.

"I do the laundry," Fred whispered.

"You do what?" Roger chuckled.

"Laugh if you must." Fred turned up his chin. "But it helps my wife, and I enjoy doing it. It feels like putting chaos back into order. We do the laundry together and then put it up in the closet. Plus, we have our best conversations right there in the laundry room. Roger, if you ever repeat this information in public, I swear . . ."

Both men laughed, and the tension of the moment disappeared.

"Go on and fold laundry then," Roger urged. "Crockett Steel can wait until tomorrow."

After Fred left, Roger forced himself to turn off his mobile phone and go home. He found Darlene and the girls in the kitchen, decorating a batch of sugar cookies. Roger washed his hands and aptly decorated one of the biggest cookies, drawing a face complete with spectacles, mustache, and earrings that got a high approval rating from the girls.

Having finished with the cookies and the kitchen cleanup, the girls went to bed, and Roger decided to turn in early and read a book. Darlene had been rather quiet all evening and withdrew to the family room to watch a movie. Before going to sleep, Roger took a quiet moment to pray for guidance and wisdom in the day ahead, and he ended by praying that Darlene would be able to put the past where it belonged and give him the chance to be the husband and father that God wanted him to be.

• • •

Roger's family woke up to a crisp morning as they settled into their newfound breakfast routine. Roger dropped the girls off at school and said a little prayer for them to have a fun and enriching day in the classroom. He rested his hands on the steering wheel as he watched the girls skip their way through the gate and onto the school yard. As he was about to pull out, there was a rap on his window. He pushed the button to roll it all the way down.

"Hey, Roger!" said a lissom young man with very white teeth.

"Oh, hi!" Roger could not remember his neighbor's name.

"Andrew," he said.

"Of course, I'm sorry," Roger said.

"No need to apologize," said Andrew. "I'm terrible with names too."

"I'll take you up on that cup of coffee whenever you have the time," Roger said.

"Oh! Great!" Andrew widened his smile. "I'm going to be out of town this weekend. How about the following Saturday morning?"

"Sure," Roger agreed.

"Great. Look forward to it." Andrew walked back to his car and waved good-bye.

Roger felt a swath of warmth lift his spirits. He was glad that he had met his neighbor; he felt a weight come off his chest. Andrew. He must remember his name next time he saw him. Andrew. Saturday next week. Maybe he could help Andrew with his business. Was this the way Bob was feeling about helping him every Monday? It felt really good.

Even though it was almost 8:00 a.m., feeling buoyant,

Roger stopped at the express car wash. While he waited in the customer lounge and sipped a glass of orange juice, he noticed a petite woman on the other side of the street, cranking out the awning as she prepared for another day of business in her little bookstore. Roger wondered whether a store like that could possibly sell enough books to pay the rent, much less provide an income for the owner. He went on to ponder the number of businesses that simply did not have a formula for success. You see them come and go, so many dreams and so much hard work vanishing into nothing for lack of good planning or attention to projected break-even points and income goals. Just a year ago, there was a gourmet ice-cream parlor in that same space. The mental escape triggered a thought as Roger silently wished the bookshop owner better luck and picked up his mobile phone to call Fred.

"Hi, Fred. It's Roger. Listen . . . sorry for the short notice, but could you bring a report to the meeting and completely break out all the income and expenses we have associated directly with Crockett? If you have time, give us some historicals for the past three years."

"No problem, boss. I'll put it together," Fred replied.

"Thank-you, Fred," Roger said. "I appreciate it."

Roger then called his assistant, Becky.

"This is Becky," the familiar voice answered.

"Good morning, Becky," Roger said. "I have an unusual

assignment for you today. Can you survey all our employees and ask them how much of their time is spent working specifically on the CS account? Also, ask them what they like best about the account and what they like least."

"No problem," said Becky.

"I apologize for the rush, Becky, but do you think you can write a summary report of the responses and have it ready for our meeting at 1:00 p.m.?" asked Roger.

"You got it," Becky assured him.

"Thank-you, Becky. I appreciate it," Roger said, and he truly meant it.

On the short drive into the office, Roger's thoughts wandered. *What would happen to Triple A if Crockett Steel were not around?* He had never thought of such a thing; he had invested so much effort in winning the account and then building a strong long-term relationship. When he got to his desk, he found Becky's survey questionnaire neatly printed out and waiting for him.

"Do I have to fill it in too?" Roger asked Becky.

"Of course," Becky answered with a smile. "You said everyone should fill it in, so I take that to include our CEO as well."

He felt a wave of gratitude for these wonderful people who came in to work every day and gave their best to the job. He obediently sat down and stared at the questionnaire. To his surprise, he didn't know how to answer it. It took him a few minutes to formulate a cohesive reply. He looked at question one: How much time did he spend on the Crockett Steel account? At least a third of his time every day went into planning or reviewing materials or putting out fires related to Crockett, so he wrote 33 percent. The second question—What did he enjoy most about working with Crockett Steel?—he left blank because he honestly could not think of one single thing that was enjoyable these days. The fun relationships that developed in the early years had been replaced by Crockett's ever-changing staff and e-mail work orders. He skipped to what he liked least and rapidly wrote, "Crockett controls my company more than I do. It has almost defined who we have become the last couple of years."

So there it was, in black and white. Roger stared at the Crockett Steel calendar with a picture of its huge corporate complex in Indianapolis and wondered whether all this discovery effort that was surfacing today could possibly be the result of his honest prayer for guidance and wisdom. He was excited about the management meeting and what he would find out with his team. The feeling reminded him of the early days of Triple A and what it felt like to work with like-minded people toward a common goal.

So this is what it feels like to enjoy work . . . I had almost forgotten.

CHAPTER**NINE**

Roger went into the meeting with a mixture of anxiety and excitement. For the last few days he had felt as if his thoughts and feelings had been put through a blender, and now he was just hoping that he would be able to make sense of whatever was coming next. A line had been drawn in the sand. Although Crockett Steel's ultimatum had caught Roger by surprise, it was to be expected that the growing tension with his company's main client would reach a critical point sooner or later. The time had come to face the difficulty of the position that Roger's company had slowly been wedged into. Roger assumed everyone's concern would be job security. He was not sure how his employees would handle talk about the possibility of not moving forward with Crockett Steel. It was time to find out.

Roger opened the door and quickly surveyed the table. There were a platter of gourmet sandwich wraps cut into dainty finger-thin slices, a selection of fruit juices, and small mineral water bottles with colorful labels that intimated the intriguing concept that the contents were so much more than what they looked like since, mainly, they all looked and tasted like water. Becky and Fred were already there as well as Keith Smith of quality control, operations manager Blake Phelps, and sales manager Lisa Brewer. Fred was occupied with his failed attempt to take one of the sandwich rolls to his mouth; it had ended in a splatter of scattered ingredients on his plate.

"Are they supposed to cut them this thin to make them easy to eat?" Fred grumbled. "I don't care how exotic the ingredients. It doesn't help much when you lose most of your sundried-tomato tapenade with mango carpaccio in midair."

"There you have it," said Quality Control Keith, "best intentions. The deli means well, but the end result is far from optimal."

"Well said, Keith." Fred nodded in agreement. "There is a Zen moment right there. Best intentions can leave you hungry."

"Or else you could say," chimed in Blake from operations, "that even when you have essentially a good thing, if you cut it too thin, it will fall apart at the worst possible moment."

Roger helped himself to the sandwiches and a bottle of apple juice.

"Or you could sum it up saying," Roger ventured, "why mess with a good thing?"

"Precisely," said Fred. "What's wrong with a regular sandwich like turkey on rye?"

"Except if your customers are ready for something different," stated Lisa, "then you might be missing an opportunity."

"So what you're saying," Roger asserted, "is that if you were a sandwich, you could suffer from being too square."

They all shook their heads as though this conversational escape had gone too far.

"Possibly," said Keith, not willing to let it go, "but you would have to be wary of the difference between change to improve and change for the sake of change, without any purpose."

"Yes," said Blake, winking, "or maybe your customers will convince you to become a round sandwich and then change their minds and want a square one again, but by then it's too late because you've already fallen apart."

"I have a feeling that we are talking about more than sandwiches here." Roger smiled while attempting to rope everyone back to reality.

Everyone laughed and started to make room for notepads and papers. Roger glanced around the table and realized that, joking aside, these people would not have a proper lunch break today. Suddenly the thought of his managers having to stuff a quick bite in a hurry to get on with the business at hand didn't seem right. It didn't seem healthy.

Roger felt a new fondness for his team, willing to forgo their personal time for the sake of Triple A, as they had done so many times recently, and doing it with a good attitude and even finding humor in it.

With great sincerity, Roger formally started the meeting: "You all know why we are here. I am asking you to openly express your thoughts and feelings about Crockett Steel. I value your comments. We have a big decision to make today."

Fred got right down to business and reviewed the profit-and-loss reports related to the Crockett Steel account over the past thirty-six months. Roger felt a pang in his stomach. The profit margin was slim, but it had helped Triple A stay afloat for years. Once they had finished going over the numbers, Roger asked everyone to share the results of the survey.

"If you don't mind, Roger," said Keith, the quality control manager who also doubled as production overseer, "I would like to say something before we get into the specifics of the survey. I think you should know that I believe that we lost two of our best employees because of Crockett Steel."

"Do you mean Eddie and D. J.?" Fred asked.

"Yes. The official story was that Eddie wanted to start his own business, and D. J. had an offer for more money closer to his home," Keith continued. "But I know that Eddie is actually helping his brother roof houses and is not very happy, and although it is true that D. J. is making a couple more thousand a year, they would have never left if they had not been miserable here dealing with one Crockett Steel fiasco after another. D. J. was the one person on the line who could go out to the customer job site and troubleshoot, but he grew tired of Crockett using him as a scapegoat when actually most of the problems came from their last-minute changes and unreasonable pressure on our lines. He felt unappreciated, and I can't really blame him."

Keith paused and thought a moment. He looked up at Fred. "Maybe you should start adding those turnover and training expenses into the Crockett pro forma, then see how we are doing."

Fred gave Roger a pensive look.

Blake spoke next.

"I never lose an opportunity to beat a dead horse," he said, "so I'll add my two cents. I spend about 40 percent of my time dealing with the Crockett account. There is always something with them every single day. When you look at the proportional allotment of my time on the CS account versus other clients, it doesn't look so good. I believe we are missing an opportunity with our smaller customers. We never get a chance to develop our business with them because we are all so busy putting out CS fires. Morale is at the lowest ever. At this point, if we give in to Crockett's request to lower our prices again, it will be a hard sell to our people on the floor to keep them motivated in that environment."

Roger slowly rubbed his forehead and turned to Lisa.

"Let's hear from sales," he said. "What do you think about this, Lisa?"

"Well," she said almost in a sigh, "from a sales perspective, it has always been nice to throw around Crockett Steel as a reference. I believe the people in management always say good things about us when they get a call for references. However . . ."

Lisa paused and looked at Keith and Blake as if to apologize for what was coming.

"I'm afraid that it sounds like operations is always behind schedule," she continued. "I miss a lot of sales because we are not able to fully commit to the production deadlines. You know that today any new account that we secure requests a guarantee of delivery. We are just not in a position to give it."

"Please tell me," said Roger, rubbing his forehead again, "that we are not losing sales because you are concerned about our production."

Lisa was silent. Blake nodded.

"I can see where Lisa is coming from," he said. "We spend a lot of time on red tape and paperwork responding to Crockett's urgent demands. When Lisa needs our help to close the other deals, I have to admit that most of the time we are less than receptive. We are just trying to keep our heads above water."

Roger sat back in his chair and stretched his legs under the table.

"Terrific," he groaned. "Let's hear about the results of the survey."

Becky retrieved her notes from a manila folder.

"As you know," she said, "the survey was put together in a very short time, so the methodology to collect the information was to give the department heads the task of collating the information from their staff. I then combined the results and wrote this short executive summary. Here it goes . . ."

Becky then quickly read the list of results. To the question, What do you like the least about Crockett Steel? the staff listed:

- Do not treat us with respect.
- Always need everything in a rush.
- Forcing us to cut prices and lower our standards.
- They micromanage, causing too much red tape.
- They require too much time from upper management.
- They've taken the fun out of working for Triple A.

For the question, What do you like the most? there were

a few scattered remarks such as *the steady revenue stream*, but most of the employees left this section blank.

Becky finished reading the executive summary and handed the paper to Roger. He set it down in front of him and looked at it a few moments. He then adjusted his chair closer to the table.

"Please thank everyone on my behalf for this feedback," Roger said, looking at his staff, "and I appreciate all your honest feedback. I know that every one of you has done your best. Based on your feedback, I am going to tell Crockett Steel that we are not able to reduce our prices. And for the time being, we will keep working with our existing agreement.

"In fact, I am going to tell them that, per our original agreement, we are going to have to pass the cost of change orders on to them. We stopped doing this a while back out of fear of losing the account. If they have change orders, we will bill them as per the agreement. If we need to send out staff to troubleshoot, we will also include that extra time on the invoice. We need to steer back toward the original intent of our contract.

"I am committed to bringing Triple A back to its original level of performance, a place that we can be proud of and enjoy working for. Whether Triple A will be able to have Crockett Steel as its main customer is still a question mark. I will let you know as soon as possible and ask that you keep moving forward in the interim."

Everyone nodded and gathered up papers.

"Roger," Blake said, "in operations we will probably ruffle some feathers at Crockett Steel when we start billing for those extra services."

"I will contact Crockett Steel personally," Roger said, "to inform them of our course of action. If anybody objects to you, just direct him to me. Becky, please give priority to these calls."

Roger left the meeting and walked back to his office. He had a new bounce in his step. He was in charge again.

CHAPTER TEN

This Monday afternoon it was Roger who arrived a few minutes before Bob in the break room for their usual meeting. He settled at the table and took advantage of the time to look over his notes in his little orange notebook. *Directive Three*, he read, *Pray; don't pout.* Had he followed it? He tried to remember. Well, he had certainly prayed for guidance after the Crockett Steel ultimatum, and he had certainly tried not to complain. Could it be that the questions he asked his staff in the questionnaire were an answer to his prayer for guidance? Or was it just a coincidence, just an idea that had crossed his mind at the right time? *That questionnaire had certainly shed light on the real nature of the situation with Triple A's main customer*, Roger reflected. At that moment, Bob arrived, carrying a small package.

"I'm sorry I'm late! I got held up. But I did bring you a present," said Bob, with his usual good humor. In fact, he was right on time.

"What's the occasion?" Roger asked as he poured two mugs of steaming green tea. He had to admit that it was an acquired taste after all; he rather liked green tea better than coffee these days.

"No particular reason. Presents are best when they are unexpected, don't you think? But first tell me about your week. How's the family doing?"

"I think we had a breakthrough this morning, but I'm not sure yet," said Roger. "You know how the girls have gotten into this new routine of me having breakfast with them and then driving them to school?"

"Yes. Sounds lovely," said Bob.

"It's a lot of fun actually. We all have cereal and fruit, and Becca always asks for an extra cereal bowl and a spoon for Chuck, her invisible friend. Except for this morning. She said that Chuck had gone to visit his aunt in California, so we wouldn't need the extra place setting. What do you think?"

"Poor Chuck!" Bob laughed. "I think that may be the end of him. I don't think he's coming back."

"Really?" asked Roger.

"Not claiming to be an expert here," Bob said, "but the thing is that Becca's imaginary friend may have been a manifestation of a sense of loneliness or an absence of someone, so she filled the hole with Chuck. Now that the balance has been restored, mainly her relationship with her father, her sense of security has probably increased; therefore, poor ol' Chuck has been forced into retirement."

"Good," Roger said. "Nothing personal, but having Chuck around was a little creepy sometimes. Darlene was so relieved that she suggested we go out to see a movie this weekend to celebrate. Just the two of us. I don't even remember the last time that we went out as a couple. Come to think of it, Bob, I think my wife asked me on a date."

"It sounds to me like you are making progress at home," observed Bob.

"Well, I owe it to you and Alice, I tell you that much," said Roger. "Now if I can only put out the fire du jour at work, I'll be all right."

Roger gave Bob a brief overview of the unnerving letter from Crockett Steel and the subsequent idea to quiz the employees before the meeting.

"It seems to me that you found the guidance you were looking for," said Bob.

"I have to admit that the quiz and the meeting were very educational," acknowledged Roger. "Here, I wrote down the findings in the back of my orange notebook. Let's see. In the questions about what they *least liked* about working with Crockett, we had a long list with some common threads: they don't treat us with respect, they are forcing us to cut prices and lower our standards, they constantly move the goalposts, they require too much paperwork and supervision to keep up with the changes, and they micromanage us. Hardly surprising because I knew all these things, but somehow seeing them in black and white in my employees' handwriting made it so clear.

"Then there was the other question, about what they *most liked* about this client. We got a few replies along the lines that they pay our bills and it is a good image to have such a big client in our portfolio, and someone wrote that they keep us on our toes about keeping our quality up and our costs down. I suppose there is truth in all of this. Particularly about keeping us on our toes, I wouldn't want to lose that. But you know what the overwhelming majority of our staff wrote about what they liked most about working with this client?"

"What?" asked Bob, leaning forward in his chair.

"Nothing," said Roger.

"Nothing," reflected Bob.

"That's it. They couldn't find one thing that they enjoyed about their work for Crockett Steel, so they left the question blank."

"That reminds me," said Bob, "in music, the rests are just as important as the notes, so the musician must count silences with the same value as the notes."

"Exactly. Those blank replies spoke louder than any words," assented Roger. "Nobody's enjoying the work anymore, and that doesn't make any sense to me."

"So you've got a case of the tail wagging the dog," Bob said.

"Absolutely," said Roger. "You know, I am so relieved that you see it the same way I do. I feared that you might have a different interpretation, with all your business experience."

"Actually," Bob said, "I think the questions you asked your staff were right on target. I don't think I would have come up with that myself. The teacher sometimes learns more than the student."

"Hardly!" Roger chuckled. "But it is so easy to get sidetracked when you are in the thick of the battle. One of the founding principles for my business was that employees should be able to find their work fulfilling. I strayed away from that, and I didn't even know it. My conversations with you have opened a new chapter for my business."

"Well, thank-you. That's such a nice thing to say. I agree, it is helpful to have someone lend you an impartial ear," said Bob, "which reminds me of what Alice gave me one day."

"That would be Directive Four?"

"Of course." Bob patted the package on the table.

"Do you mean this is what Alice gave you?" Roger asked.

"Right." Bob nodded.

"But I couldn't possibly accept it. It's Alice's gift to you," protested Roger.

"Alice would be delighted," Bob said, pushing the package across the table. "Open it."

Roger hesitated a moment, then took the package and opened it carefully. Inside there was a black silk box, and what he saw when he opened it took his breath away. There, appearing to give off its own gleaming light, was an exquisite men's gold watch. Each delicate hand was crowned with a tiny sparkling diamond, and a third diamond dotted the Roman numeral XII at the top. The face contained a discreet engraving that said simply, "Pass it around." Roger was speechless.

"Quite something, isn't it?" Bob beamed proudly.

"Alice gave it to you?" Roger kept asking the same question.

**Directive 4:
Pass it
around.**

"Yep. Alice knew I loved watches. I never had any penchant for other kinds of jewelry, but for some reason, I always stopped to look at watches in shop windows. Still do. When things started going really well for us—I had recovered from my hospital scare, work was prospering, and our family was thriving—Alice wanted to give me something to remind me that there were others who had a need to learn from my experiences and to hear the directives that I had received from her. And so she had this watch specially engraved for me. It is a beautiful thing. Every time I looked at my watch, I was reminded that time was flying, and I should be sharing my knowledge and wisdom with others before it was too late. This is what I've been doing ever since, like I'm doing now with you."

"So this is Directive Four? *Pass it around*?" asked Roger, thinking for an instant of his neighbor Andrew and their coffee appointment coming up Saturday morning. That would be a great chance for him to possibly share or "pass around" some personal experiences and maybe even these same directives he was receiving from Bob.

"Yes." Bob grinned. "Simple, isn't it? Why don't you try it on? You may need to have the band adjusted for size."

"Oh, no!" Roger protested again. "There is no way I could possibly accept this, Bob! It must be worth a fortune!"

"It's worth more than a fortune," admitted Bob with a smile. "It's priceless. When Alice gave it to me, I found the true purpose of my life—to help others find their way back to themselves and their families, and most of all, to find their way back to God. You can't put a price on finding your purpose in life!"

"Exactly," said Roger. "I can't accept such a gift, especially knowing what it means to you."

"But that is exactly why I am giving it to you," Bob stated. "Because it means so much to me is precisely the reason why you should accept it. Anyone can give a meaningless gift. That would be no great reflection on my character, would it?"

"But aren't you going to wear it?" Roger said, still resisting.

"I have no occasion to wear it nowadays," said Bob. "Besides, my hands have gotten so bony that it keeps slipping off. I'm afraid I'll lose it. I want you to have it."

Bob's thin, spotted hands were visibly shaking, and he looked at Roger with such affection and such pleading in his eyes that Roger was pressed into accepting.

"I'll tell you what," said Roger. "I'll wear it for a few weeks, just to honor your amazing generosity, but then you'll have to accept it back."

"How many weeks will you wear it?" asked Bob, narrowing his eyes.

"I don't know. How many more directives do we still have?"

Bob checked his little orange notebook.

"Let's see . . ." Bob paused. "We are on Directive Four now . . . there are six in total, so we only have two more to go. Pretty good progress, Roger!"

"Okay. I'll wear the watch for two weeks, and then you'll take it back," Roger said.

"I promise I'll take it back only if you still want me to," Bob said.

"Fair enough," Roger said, slipping the watch on his wrist.

Both men admired the gold watch settled snuggly against Roger's strong, tanned wrist.

"It fits perfectly!" said Roger with surprise.

"It most certainly does," agreed Bob. "So what are you going to do about that Crockett client of yours?"

"I'm still working on it," said Roger, "but I may have to take a lesson from Becca and send my client to visit an aunt in California, like Chuck did."

"Yes!" Bob laughed. "A long trip on a one-way ticket!"

CHAPTER ELEVEN

Breathing in the clear air of the brisk Saturday morning, Roger walked casually over to his neighbor's house. Through the kitchen glass door, he could see his neighbor Andrew bent intently over a sheaf of papers on the kitchen table. Roger rapped on the glass.

"Come in!" Andrew waved.

"Good morning. Did I interrupt your work?" Roger asked.

"It would be rather difficult to find me at a time when I'm not working!" Andrew let out a nervous laugh. "Except maybe when I'm sleeping, and I'm not doing much of that lately."

"I know the feeling," Roger said.

Other than the mountain of paperwork on the table, the kitchen was impeccably clean and tidy, with stainless-steel appliances and yellow and white striped curtains. Andrew poured two mugs of coffee and brushed the papers aside with his elbow to clear the table. He folded his notebook computer shut and placed it on the papers as a paperweight. He got a small plate of brownies and offered one to Roger.

"Missy made them," Andrew said.

"Mmm. Delicious," Roger said, tasting the brownie, and then nodded toward the stack of papers. "Are you sure you're not too busy? I can come back later after I finish mowing my lawn."

"Nah. I need to take a break, actually," said Andrew.

"Is it a busy time of year for you?" Roger asked.

"It's like this all the time now." Andrew sighed. "Unfortunately, it's not reflected in my results. I wish we were making as much money as the amount of time that I'm putting into it."

"So tell me about your business," Roger said.

Andrew described how he had worked for a few years for a marketing and promotions company. He had learned on the job how to produce quality, inexpensive promotional items. After he married Missy, he suddenly decided to quit his job and start his own company.

"Missy was nervous about the decision," Andrew admitted, "but I thought, *How hard can it be? I already know a lot about the market.* Now I'm beginning to think that Missy was right. Making the products is a piece of cake for me, but getting clients to trust me and place a first order is a whole different ball game."

"Would you mind if I ask you a very personal question?"

"Go ahead," said Andrew, sipping his coffee.

"How is Missy feeling these days about the business?" Roger asked.

Andrew's jaw tightened as he set his coffee cup down.

"That is a bit of a sticky subject," Andrew replied. "Missy is usually a very positive person. But lately she has adopted this 'I told you so' attitude. Which doesn't help since I already feel like a toad. It's more than that, if I'm perfectly honest. I think that the stalemate in the business has tainted our relationship. When we got married, we both were eager to start a family, but then I asked Missy to put the baby plans on hold until the business got established. You know, kids are a big responsibility, and I wanted to have a solid footing before bringing children into the equation."

"And I'm guessing Missy is not too happy about that?" Roger asked.

"Nope." Andrew shook his head slowly from side to side. "Not happy at all. One day a few weeks ago I asked her if there was anything she regretted in her life. Normally she would just say nothing at all. You know, Missy is the type of person who always looks forward. That day she simply said that she regretted starting the business. But I really believe that she may be regretting marrying me. She is not happy.

"At first she kept reminding me that I had agreed to have children when we got married. I think she felt that I betrayed our agreement. Now it's even worse. She just doesn't mention it anymore. She barely talks to me. She had to go back to work to help with the expenses, so that has put any thoughts of having a baby even further into the background. It has to be difficult for her, but I don't really know what to do. I really believe it would be irresponsible of me to start a family in this situation. Plus we are both tired and grumpy all the time, so it is not exactly a romantic environment anyway."

"I'm sorry if I'm stirring up a painful subject," Roger said.

"Not at all," Andrew said. "I admire your success, and I very much appreciate your interest in helping me out."

Roger paused. He wondered how he was going to help Andrew when he was actually trying to figure out his own situation. He also wondered whether Bob had any of these doubts in his own mind when he started mentoring Roger. Everybody has his own worries. Bob had found a way to set them aside and find the time and the inclination to help others, which was a much better way to spend your time than being immersed in your own problems. Maybe there was a key there somewhere. If Roger could concentrate fully on Andrew's situation, even for one hour, he could help not only Andrew but also himself at the same time. Bob's words made more and more sense each day that passed. Roger didn't feel confident enough to deal directly with Andrew's relationship problems, so instead he chose to discuss the matter that he knew best, the challenges Andrew was facing in his work life.

"What could be the root of the trouble with your business? Do you think you overestimated the demand for your products?" Roger asked.

"No! That's what's so painful. The demand is there. It is huge and continuously growing. What I didn't realize is that for this type of product, advertising alone is not enough. Most of the clients come from referrals. Someone sees the pens or key chains or whatever and asks the business owners, 'Where do you get these made?' They say, 'You should see so-and-so and tell him I sent you,' and so forth. I have spent a small fortune advertising in the yellow pages and newspapers, and I have blanketed the area with cold calls, but if I can't get the word of mouth going, I'm going to be drowning really soon. Did you have a rough time when you started Triple A?"

"Rough is not the word. But I was fortunate to have some good people to go to for advice. I still do. So what you really need is just a baseline client that can get you started," said Roger.

"Exactly," said Andrew, "and then it happens really quickly. One client leads to another. In my old job they had figured out that one good client gets you an average of seven new clients through referrals. But how am I going to get those first clients? I'm caught in a loop."

Roger and Andrew discussed the different options for assistance available for small businesses through local organizations. Andrew showed Roger his expenses, the advertising campaign in detail, and samples of the products. Roger was impressed and made a few remarks and suggestions on how to make the ads stand out even more.

"You know what?" Roger said after a pause. "I think you are doing an excellent job here." He thought about how much money Triple A spent every year on advertising specialties. "Why don't you give me a brochure? I'll take it with me to the office."

"That would be fantastic. Thank-you!" said Andrew, handing him a few brochures and some samples.

Roger looked at the well-laid-out brochures: ASAP—Advertising Specialties by Andrew Palms.

"ASAP. That's a good name," said Roger with an encouraging smile. "I'll let you keep working now. I'm going to do some yard work, and then my wife is taking me to see a movie, so I have to scrub up and get myself presentable."

"Your wife is taking you?" Andrew laughed. "Uh-oh . . . what are you going to see?"

"I'm afraid Darlene is picking the movie, so it will be something romantic and emotional!" Roger laughed too. "I just hope it's not a musical!"

"I love musicals," Andrew admitted.

"You are not serious," Roger declared.

"Yep." Andrew nodded. "And Missy can't stand them."

They both laughed. Roger realized that he hadn't said anything to Andrew in relation to his personal difficulties; they had talked mainly about the business. It didn't come naturally to discuss emotional aspects of his life, let alone somebody else's. Roger turned toward the door and paused. He turned back to face his neighbor.

"You know, Andrew, what you were saying about your wife, Missy?"

Roger paused as Andrew nodded in acknowledgment.

"I'm not one to give advice on these things," Roger continued, "especially since we hit a rough patch in our marriage too."

"You did?" Andrew looked surprised.

"Absolutely," Roger said. "I know that it may sound like a cliché, but do you think Missy sees the light at the end of the tunnel?"

"I don't think so," Andrew replied flatly.

"Listen, as I said, I am not the right person to give marital advice," said Roger, "but for what it's worth, here it goes—tell her that you love her; remind her of how much she means to you."

"She means everything to me," Andrew said.

"Then tell her that all the hard work is going to pay off,"

Roger stated, "and that you are more excited about your future together now than ever before. Focus on *your family's* future and not the future of the business. Remember that the business exists only to help you achieve the goals that you have set in your personal lives. The business doesn't exist to control you, but to enable you."

"Do you think she'll listen?" Andrew asked.

"I think you'll be amazed," Roger said, then winked as he turned to leave. "Let's just call it *good habits for married entrepreneurs!*"

As Andrew seemed to be sponging up the good advice, Roger himself was amazed at how well that might work. He found it ironic to hear himself say those words.

"I really enjoyed our conversation," said Andrew with a big grin. "I'm so glad you stopped by."

"I tell you what," said Roger, looking at his newly acquired watch, "I'll come by this same time next Saturday if you are free, and I'll share some advice from a friend of mine who happened to help me a great deal. Who knows? Maybe you'll find it interesting too. It's just six simple principles . . . doesn't take long at all."

"Absolutely," Andrew said. "I'll have the coffee ready."

"See you then!" Roger waved and walked back home.

In the front yard Darlene and Sarah were helping Becca take off the training wheels from her little bike.

"Look, Daddy!" she said as she rode by on the sidewalk. "I'm riding like a big girl!"

"Looking good!" said Roger as he brushed a kiss on the back of his wife's neck, a familiar gesture that he had not repeated for a while now.

Roger was surprised to recognize that the small family rituals that had become so difficult and unnatural had now begun to flow easily again.

"Isn't she clever?" Darlene said. "We took off her training wheels, and she just rode into the wind."

"They grow up too fast," Roger said. "No more Chuck, it seems?"

"No mention of Chuck." Darlene giggled. "That's one less invisible mouth to feed."

Roger applied the rest of the morning to mowing the lawn and tidying up his tools. After a light lunch, he set up his laptop computer on the garden table and typed out a few e-mails to his staff. He was impressed to find that his neighbor Andrew had immediately followed up their conversation with an e-mail including some price listings for specialty items. Roger forwarded the e-mail to Becky, asking her to include the price listings in her comparison with her usual suppliers for the next order of Triple A Christmas giveaway items. He played with the girls in the garden and then got ready for his date with Darlene. He came back downstairs wearing a blue jacket over a freshly pressed denim shirt, Darlene's favorite outfit for him, and patting a little package in his pocket.

Darlene was getting the girls ready for a sleepover with Grandma, and both girls were so excited, they could hardly wait to get in the car. As the girls bolted out the door, Roger took Darlene's hand and gently held her back. She looked lovely in her black cropped pants and a fuchsia silk top, he thought with pride. Darlene turned her eyes up to Roger with mild surprise. He presented her with the little package in his pocket, and she blushed youthfully as she looked down at the sparkling pair of earrings.

"Roger!" she gasped. "They are gorgeous!"

She pressed a kiss on his cheek and then a second, slower kiss on his lips.

"Do you really like them?" Roger asked, helping her put on the new earrings.

"Are you kidding?" Darlene said, looking at her reflection in the hall mirror. "I love them!"

"I know that the last few months have been particularly difficult," Roger said, "and I'm sorry that I let things get to that point."

"Yes," said Darlene, "it's been hard . . . but we're getting better. I was so worried that we would get to a place where we wouldn't be able to turn back, you know, too far away from each other."

"You were right all the time," Roger said. "It just took me a while to understand. And I love you," he added, urgently pressing her hand, "forever."

Darlene nodded silently and smiled.

CHAPTER TWELVE

H ello, Roger!" Bob called out cheerfully. "How was your week?"

Roger sat down at the break-room table across from Bob and jiggled the gold watch on his wrist.

"I've been very stylish this past week," Roger announced. "I've received quite a number of compliments on your watch, I must tell you."

"You should keep it then." Bob laughed and passed Roger a steaming mug of green tea.

"It's coming back to you next week," Roger said, tapping on the face of the watch.

They both took out their little orange notebooks, as Roger told Bob about his meeting with Andrew and how he planned to share Directive One with him this week.

"Let me check my notes," said Roger, studying his notebook. "Ah! Yes. Very interesting. After meeting with the staff and then forever crunching numbers with Fred, our CFO, we have decided we are not going to reduce our pricing, and that may well mean that our biggest client, Crockett Steel, will be lost to the competition."

"Quite a bold decision indeed," remarked Bob.

"We are choking ourselves with this client. The company demands more and more discounts, but at the same time increases our costs by last-minute change orders and interminable paperwork. Yes, it was a very difficult decision to make, but now it's done."

"Have you informed Crockett Steel yet?" Bob asked.

"I happened to meet the CEO at a charity event the other night, and we had an informal talk, so I guess you can say that the cat's out of the bag."

"Have you seen any reaction yet?" Bob asked.

"Not yet," Roger replied. "In fact, the weekly purchase orders came in electronically right on schedule, but it may take the company some time to turn over to another supplier. It is a huge organization."

"Maybe the company won't change suppliers," suggested Bob.

"Perhaps," said Roger, "but I'm not going to count on it. As I said to the staff, we have enough smaller clients to break even. If we concentrate on growing our business with them, instead of putting all our energy into one big client, we are going to be okay. I've learned my lesson. I'm not going to let one client dominate my company ever again."

"Maybe Crockett will call your bluff," said Bob, "to see if you mean it or if you're just playing tough."

"Oh, it's not a bluff. We mean it all right," Roger emphasized. "The news went down so well with our staff that it was quite a shock. There was a festive atmosphere. You would have thought we had just signed a big customer, not said good-bye to one. Do you know what they did?"

"What?" asked Bob.

"They sent me a giant cookie, and they wrote with icing 'Triple A rocks! The best is yet to come . . .'"

"That's wonderful!" Bob chuckled.

"I almost cried with relief when I saw that cookie." Roger laughed. "I set it on a table and we all shared a piece. We talked and joked, and then everyone went back to work with enthusiasm. It felt just like when we started the company. It felt great. They even seemed excited about filling the remaining Crockett orders we had. Fred said the employees like working for me, and it was reassuring for them to know that I—not Crockett Steel—was back in charge of their future employment."

"I'm almost thinking that you've been getting ahead and already implementing Directive Five," said Bob.

"Really?" asked Roger.

"Have you by any chance . . ." Bob said, narrowing his eyes playfully, "been reading Alice's directives behind my back?"

"Oh, boy!" Roger laughed. "I'm seriously curious now. What does Directive Five say?"

"Very simple, really," Bob answered. "Directive Five says: Don't spend; invest!"

Bob paused a moment to let Roger absorb the statement.

"Alice was a careful spender, you see," Bob continued, "even when we were more than comfortable. But the directive doesn't refer only to financial resources. It is much broader than that. Alice was a firm believer that we must evaluate all our activities in life as either an investment or an expense. Whenever she would see me stressed-out over things that were not that important, she would whisper, 'Don't spend; invest.'"

Directive 5: Don't spend; invest!

"I don't understand," Roger remarked in a tone of voice encouraging Bob to continue.

"It is really simple," Bob explained, "so simple, in fact, that you are already doing it—you just haven't thought about it in those terms. You must pause and reflect on your activity and the brain time that you are putting into a task or decision. Then you play the tape forward a bit to see where all this work and stress is leading. Then you ask yourself whether the eventual outcome has any *significance*. You can take it a step further and ask yourself whether the outcome could have any *eternal significance*."

"Eternal significance?" Roger repeated.

"You've heard the cliché that you only live once," Bob continued. "Well, Alice and I happened to believe that it is true. We both believed that since you pass through this earth only once, it is important to make a difference. We figured out that God made each of us for a reason—for a purpose, as we were saying last week. Our biggest challenge in life is to try to understand and fulfill that purpose. It is like our job assignment on how we will serve God while we are here. We used to say that our aspiration was, when the time came to meet the 'Big CEO' in heaven, for Him to take one look at us and say, 'Well done, good and faithful servant!'"

"Sounds great," said Roger, "but what if we don't know what our purpose is?"

"It is very common to spend our energy focusing on our own agendas," said Bob, "but if we leave our slates blank and listen, we often find that God is speaking to us loud and clear. Our purpose in life is not complicated or hard to understand. It is very easy to find. But we are not likely to listen when we spend our whole lives focused on our own agendas, not His agenda.

"It is easy to tell the difference. Usually when we are focused on our own agendas, we are spending. We spend our time, money, talent, and so forth. But when we are focused on our God-given purpose, we are investing. So what has helped me over the years, when I get all caught up in some work activity, is to simply stop and ask myself whose agenda am I focused on. Is there some *eternal significance* in what I am doing? Does the outcome of my activity or the process I am going through during this activity help fulfill the purpose that God created me for? Does it have any eternally significant impact on someone else?"

"You said you thought I was already implementing Directive Five," said a slightly confused Roger, "but I can't see how anything we do here at Triple A could eternally affect anyone. It is not as if we are a humanitarian company sending food to feed the hungry. I'm thinking that this may be one directive that just doesn't apply to my case."

"Ah! You are not easily persuaded." Bob sighed with a theatrical roll of his eyes. "I like that. It is good to ask the question as long as you are open to receive the answer. Allow me to illustrate. Look back at your relationship with Crockett Steel. You have told me that you decided to move your company ahead without this customer if necessary. Why?"

"Well, as I said," explained Roger, "there were many reasons, but mostly we were not making any real money, especially when we factored in all the time and effort going into keeping that client happy and meeting all its demands, distracting us away from all our other clients. The opportunity cost was enormous. Plus, morale was down in the company, and as I was telling you before, enthusiasm has never been higher since the announcement."

"Right." Bob nodded with emphasis. "That's it. For the last couple of years, you were *spending* time and money trying to grow your company with Crockett Steel. But now you have shifted gears and are focused on *investing* your time and money on the right customers, building relationships, and seeking opportunities. You took a huge step when you sent out that simple questionnaire to your staff. You were considering what was important to your employees and their families. It sounds like a lot of people were suffering but not saying much about it. My guess is that your decision not to lower your prices for Crockett Steel may have helped many employees not only at work but at home as well. They do not have to take the burden of an unfulfilled job or the aggravation of working for a customer who does not appreciate the product of their work. They may actually be able to start experiencing their families as a blessing now. And you told me yourself that they seem to be reinvigorated about work."

"Absolutely," Roger said. "The atmosphere at work is charged with energy."

"How about that?" Bob slapped the table with satisfaction. "Now, in hindsight, I would say that it was a *significant* decision. I'll take it even further and say that it was *eternally significant*. Roger, you're a Christian. It is not unreasonable to assume that a good number of people know this. Your employees are watching every move you make. If they think the only thing that makes you tick is to make the next dollar, they may never want any part of the God you serve. But when they see you choose their health and happiness over your biggest customer, then a powerful message is sent through the ranks. You have a higher calling in business. You are going to put all your efforts into turning a profit, but not at the expense of the well-being of your team. Do you see?"

"I see," said Roger.

"I say," Bob announced, "that your business is a tool that God has given you so that you will use it to fulfill His purpose in your life."

"Somehow," Roger said, "and I'm not sure exactly how we got to this point, what you just said makes a lot of sense to me. It gave me goose bumps."

"Funny you say that," noted Bob, "because when I started thinking of my purpose in life, I felt a little scared. I mean, it was a great responsibility to talk about these directives and to pass this knowledge around. I used to question my motivation. Who was I to preach these directives as if I knew better than anyone else? But then Alice would remind me that we only have so much time available on this earth, and we never know when we are going to leave it, so we might as well invest our time in things that have value. Just like the time you invested with your neighbor Andrew. I suspect you'll find that you are having a great impact on that young man's life. That is an excellent *investment* as far as I am concerned."

"Which reminds me," said Roger with feeling, "that I haven't thanked you for all your help. You've certainly made an enormous positive impact in my life, both with my family and in my business."

"That's such a nice thing to say." Bob smiled kindly. "I've enjoyed every minute."

The two men cleared the table and shook hands fondly.

"Next week is the last directive, I guess," Roger said. "But I hope that we'll continue with our chats. I'd love for you to come over and visit my family; they can't wait to meet you."

"I'd be delighted to meet them too," Bob replied. "They sound like a spirited bunch. My kind of people."

"Settled. We'll meet here Monday, and then we'll go home for dinner," said Roger.

"Maybe the following week would be best," Bob suggested. "I'm scheduled to go in for an operation, so they'll probably put me on a bland diet for a few days afterward."

"An operation?" Roger said with slight alarm. "Is there something wrong?"

"Oh, no." Bob waved his hand dismissively. "Just routine care and maintenance. I'll be in and out the same day."

"If there's anything I can do . . ." Roger offered.

"Thank-you," said Bob, "but it's really nothing. I'll be here on Monday at our usual time."

"Great. See you Monday." Roger waved and added, "Take it easy after that operation!"

"God bless you," said Bob.

CHAPTER THIRTEEN

t was a bright and sunny Saturday morning. Roger headed over to Andrew's house around 10:00 a.m. for their newly established weekly chat.

"Roger!" Andrew exclaimed as he opened the door. "I am so grateful for the order from Triple A. I can't thank you enough!"

"Oh?" said Roger. "Did Becky already place an order?"

"Yes," said Andrew, pouring two mugs of coffee. "She called me, and she said that our prices were competitive, so she faxed me an order the same day."

"I'm glad to hear that," Roger said with a laugh, "although you have nothing to thank me for. I just passed on your information, and you did the rest."

"I'll thank you anyway." Andrew pulled out a plate of cookies. "That order gave me so much energy, I'm charged up. Missy is at work, and because she couldn't be here to thank you, she made these heart-shaped almond cookies for you and your family."

Roger took one bite and smiled with pleasure.

"These cookies are fantastic!" he exclaimed. "And the brownies last week were amazing. You know, if the ad specialty business doesn't work out, you could always open a gourmet bakery!"

"I'd go bankrupt in a week. I'd eat all the inventory!" Andrew laughed. "But now please tell me about these directives. I'm bursting with curiosity."

Roger pulled out his little orange notebook. "I have a friend, Bob, who has been sharing these directives with me to help me learn how to enjoy both my personal life and my business life.

"Well, they are really Alice's directives," clarified Roger. "Alice was Bob's late wife. Let's see. Here's Directive One: Recharge versus discharge. Let me tell you how that one worked for Bob, and then I'll tell you how it worked for me . . ."

Roger invested an hour talking to his very receptive audience. He told Andrew about the night when he had been feeling so tired and blank and how reading *Living Beyond the Limits* had left him feeling full of new purpose and revitalized with energy.

"You know," Roger said, "reading about other people's selfless journeys of discovery of the human spirit makes you want to experience it for yourself. There is a multiplying effect of those stories. They not only do their good directly to the people who have been affected by their immediate actions, but they also have an incredibly wide and large inspirational effect on others.

"It's like Bob's directives, which originally came from Alice, and now are coming from me to you. They are simple principles that can change your life in a positive and fundamental way. When I was at the darkest stage of my professional and personal difficulties, I felt as if something really big had to happen in order for me to be able to fix everything that was spinning so quickly out of control. But now I know that even the smallest gesture, the slightest change in the right direction, creates an adjustment in your condition. Ever since my first conversation with Bob, I can't say that I have undertaken any radical, earth-shaking shifts in behavior, but rather gentle and subtle changes in intention. The extraordinary improvement that happened has surprised me more than anybody, believe me."

"It's interesting that you say that," Andrew observed, "because I never would have guessed that you were going through any of it. It is so encouraging to me that you have found a way to incorporate this wisdom that you have received because it makes me feel that there is hope for Missy and me."

"I know it is not easy for you," Roger said, "but all I ask is that you keep our weekly appointments and learn all the directives. It's that simple."

"You got it," Andrew declared.

After agreeing to meet again at the same time the following week, Roger walked back to the house, carrying the plate with Missy's delicious cookies. He felt an ease in his step, more comfortable with himself and his thoughts than he had been for a very long time. He went into the kitchen and set the plate of cookies on the counter where Darlene and the girls were busy with preparations for lunch. The two girls were wearing little flowered aprons and had their hands elbow deep in a mixing bowl. Roger got his barbecue tools ready and headed out to the patio.

After a while, he heard the sound of a car slowing down. Roger saw a shiny silver luxury car stop at his driveway and half expected it to contain a lost driver who wanted directions. He was surprised to see that the imposing vehicle produced none other than the CEO of Crockett Steel, Barton Woods. Roger felt a pang of apprehension, hoping that Barton would not want to rehash the discussion about the price cuts. Roger was not in the mood to interrupt his family time; now that he had worked out a balance, he was intending to keep it that way.

"Hey . . ." Roger called out, "what are you doing in this neck of the woods?"

"Oh, I don't know," said Barton. "Just driving around on a beautiful Saturday morning, took a wrong turn, and what do you know . . . I washed up on your driveway."

"Well, it's your lucky day because I just fired up the grill," said Roger, "but the girls are making the hamburgers, so I'm not guaranteeing results."

The two men shook hands, and both had a quiet sense of acknowledging the awkwardness of the unscheduled Saturday meeting.

Darlene hugged Barton and ushered him to a comfortable chair on the patio, and the two girls shyly said hello and returned to the kitchen. When Darlene went back inside to get the salads, Barton took the opportunity to address their business issue.

"You know, Roger," said Barton gravely, "I'm under a lot of pressure to compete with international pricing. We are trying to expand in Europe. You know the drill."

"Sure," said Roger, "it's very competitive."

"Right," said Barton, "so naturally my guys are always looking at the bottom line, bless them. They work hard and sometimes get a little carried away."

"How do you mean?" Roger asked.

"I guess what I'm trying to say," admitted Barton, "is that I'm not really proud of the direction we have been taking lately. It seems like all the fun has been sucked out of it. Do you know what I mean?"

"I understand more than you can imagine," said Roger. "We were having the same problem. Listen, Barton, there's no need to explain. You have your decisions to make, and I have mine, and we both have our good reasons. I'm sorry it didn't work out in a way that would allow us to keep working together, but let's not dwell on it."

"That's exactly what I wanted to talk about. The reason I came over today is that there are some things that can't be said over the phone," explained Barton. "What I want you to know is that I've always admired the way you conduct business. You have a great head on your shoulders, you are a man of character, and you've built a brilliant company."

"Thank-you!" said Roger with mild surprise.

"Well, it's the truth," declared Barton, "and I am not going to beat around the bush. We've been working together for ages now, and we've built a solid relationship. I trust you and your team of people. I've had a good talk with my guys and reminded them of all this and told them not to forget that Triple A was a big factor in bringing our company to the success that we enjoy today."

"I appreciate it, Barton," Roger said. "You know I feel the same way about Crockett Steel. Whatever has happened recently, I'll always be grateful for your trust in me when you gave me my first big break. If you are worrying about any hard feelings, I can assure you that's not the case."

"I'm glad you feel that way," Barton said, "because what I'm saying is that Crockett won't be taking our business anywhere. We are going to make sure that we continue to work with you and keep finding the best way to do business together."

Roger choked on his iced tea with surprise at the same time that Darlene was coming back with the salads. The two girls emerged and sat down at the table.

"Are you okay, honey?" Darlene asked Roger.

"I'm more than okay," said Roger. "Barton, I'm speechless. I was expecting you to go to the lowest bidder."

"We almost did," Barton said, "but then I had this heavy feeling about it, you know? It literally gave me a stomachache."

"I am very happy to hear that!" Roger laughed.

"Go ahead; I deserve it," said Barton. "I really don't know what happened. I used to enjoy my work so much. I was always itching with ideas. Now I almost dread going to the office in the morning."

"It sounds to me," said Darlene with a wink to Roger, "that he would enjoy meeting Bob."

Roger laughed heartily.

"Who's Bob?" Barton asked.

"Darlene's right," Roger said. "I met Bob just over a month ago when I was feeling exactly the way you are describing. Bob is the office janitor at Triple A, and he gave me such good advice. You would love to meet him."

"The janitor?" parroted Barton.

Roger nodded.

"The janitor gave you business advice?" repeated Barton.

"You'd have to meet Bob to understand," said Roger. "I'm seeing him on Monday, so I'll tell him about you. I'm sure he'd be delighted to meet you."

"Hey," said Barton, "if he helped you, I'm all for it."

"Barton," said Roger with a bright smile, "let me say how happy I am with your gesture today. I'm so glad you came to see me. You've taken a huge weight off my shoulders. Like you said, we have enjoyed working with Crockett Steel, and then suddenly it had all become so forced and stressful for everybody involved. I can guarantee that our team will be excited to hear the news. They may be a little leery at first, so be prepared, but I know they'll get behind it. I can't wait to tell Fred on Monday. It will knock him out of his chair. Now we'd better dig into these burgers before I turn them into charcoal!"

Roger looked around the table. There were Darlene, his best friend and the love of his life, glowing and smiling at him; their two girls, tucking hungrily into their food; and his longtime business associate, who had just paid him the biggest compliment imaginable. Roger felt very, very blessed indeed and said a silent *thank-You* to God for blessing his family and his business and for putting Bob in his path.

"By the way," Roger said to Barton as they were enjoying

coffee and heart-shaped cookies for dessert, "I'm really impressed with that car of yours. Quite the status symbol."

"Maybe," Barton responded with a laugh, "but how about that gold watch of yours for status? That thing must have cost as much as my car!"

"Actually," said Roger, "that belongs to Bob, the friend I was telling you about. He just wants me to wear it for a few days as a reminder of one of his lessons."

"A janitor who gives business advice and a gold watch!" said Barton with amusement. "That's someone I definitely have to meet."

"You will." Roger nodded. "You will."

CHAPTER FOURTEEN

Out of the corner of his eye, Roger caught sight of the janitor's cart. It was parked outside the conference room. A tall, skinny man in the janitorial company uniform emerged from the conference room and picked up a spray cleaner from the cart. He greeted Roger and continued with his task. Roger stood by the door, hesitating a moment.

"Are you helping Bob tonight?" Roger said.

"Who?" asked the man.

"Bob Tidwell . . . he cleans our office every Monday," Roger replied.

"Oh, no," said the man casually. "They called me to fill in for him today. I guess he couldn't make it."

"Is he all right?" Roger asked.

"I don't know," said the man. "I'm just the replacement. I can call the office if you like."

"No, that's okay," said Roger. "You're busy. Don't let me interrupt you."

Roger went back to his office, cleared his desktop, and

shut off his computer mechanically. Something was bothering him in the pit of his stomach. Bob was not likely to forget about their Monday appointment; he seemed to look forward to it as much as Roger did. It was not like Bob to just not show up without a message or a phone call. Roger decided to call Bob's employer, Pop's Cleaning Service, to find out the reason for Bob's absence. He found the number on Becky's Rolodex and said a silent thank-you for Becky's being so well organized.

"Pop's Cleaning Service, may I help you?" a melodious voice answered.

Roger introduced himself and asked about Bob. The woman on the phone put him on hold to find out the information.

"Mr. Bob is out sick, so we called in a replacement to Triple A today. Did the replacement not show up?"

"Yes, he did. It's not that," said Roger. "The replacement started working right on time. It's just that I was worried about Bob."

"I'm sorry. That's all I know." The voice seemed impressed by the customer's caring attitude. "Is there anything else I can help you with?"

"Well," said Roger hesitantly, "no, thank-you. You've been very kind."

"Have a nice evening, Mr. Kimbrough," she said and started to hang up.

"It's just . . ." Roger interrupted, "we became good friends, you see, and he mentioned something about an operation. I was just wondering if he's all right."

"Oh," said the voice, pausing. "Let me see if anybody here knows anything more."

After a long moment on hold, another voice came back.

"Sorry about the wait, Mr. Kimbrough," a male voice said. "It's James Norman here. I'm the 'Pop' in Pop's Cleaning Service. I hear you're inquiring after Bob."

Roger explained that he and Bob had become friends and Bob had offered his assistance and that he was concerned when Bob did not show up at their regular meeting.

"I hope I'm not getting him in trouble with you!" said Roger finally.

"Hardly," replied Norman. "I can understand how you like Bob so much. He helped me straighten out my company about eight years ago, and he even joined my staff although, as you may know, he was overly qualified. He said he liked cleaning up the business world. I'm sorry to be the bearer of bad news, but Bob is in the hospital. I saw him this morning, but I should warn you he wasn't doing too well. He's over at Methodist downtown if you care to visit."

Roger thanked the kind man profusely with all the enthusiasm he could muster and even remembered to praise the quality of Pop's Cleaning Service before he said good-bye.

Roger dashed out to his car. On his way to Methodist Hospital, he called Darlene and told her about Bob. She immediately offered to go to the hospital with Roger, knowing his phobia of all things medical. Roger was not scared of hospitals for his own sake. Rather, he had a deep-rooted unease about thinking that one of these days, the call could come, and it could be about Darlene, his parents, or—heaven forbid—one of his daughters. He swept the thought aside, feeling tiny beads of cold sweat gathering in the crease of his neck. He thanked Darlene but told her to stay with the girls and tuck them into bed. He checked in at the reception desk and was directed to the main ward where, after some asking around, he found Bob's room. He opened the door slowly, and a nurse waved him in.

"Is he asleep?" Roger whispered, not daring to look fully at Bob yet.

"You can come in," the nurse whispered, pointing to the head of the bed. "He is in and out of his sleep. I'll check on him in a few minutes. Call me if you need me. There's a buzzer over there on the left."

As she slipped noiselessly out of the room, Roger's eyes adjusted to the semidarkness. The top half of the bed was elevated at an angle, and Bob lay with his eyes closed, breathing in and out with his chest. He looked small and pale, sunk in the bed with a number of monitors and thin tubes connected to his arms and chest. Roger sat down in a chair in the corner, his head bowed down. He was hoping the nurse or a doctor would come in and tell him what was wrong with Bob. He wanted to do something that could help in some way. Roger closed his eyes and started to pray.

Roger's eyes opened as the light in the room turned suddenly much brighter. To his amazement, Bob was looking back at him, eyes opened and a faint grin on his face. The change of light had come from the bedside reading lamp, which Bob turned on.

"Were you praying for me?" Bob asked, his cheerful voice sounding slightly shaky.

"Yes," Roger admitted as he moved to the chair by Bob's bed.

"Thank-you," Bob said.

"Can I get you anything? How are you feeling?" Roger asked.

"I'm not sure," said Bob, stopping to catch his breath. "According to the doctors, I should be feeling much worse than I am. Apparently my body has gotten tired of fighting this disease for so many years. I'm all worn out inside. The operation was just too much for my tired bones."

"But . . ." Roger said. He felt his eyes watering in spite of his efforts to appear calm.

"Don't be sad for me, Roger," Bob said. "I'm not sad. My

family and my friends have made my life so rich, and Alice, who could ask for more? In fact, my whole family is here. I had to force them to go out and get something to eat. I am very blessed. You'll know what I mean when you get to be my age."

"No," protested Roger, "you'll live many more years. Don't sound like you're giving up."

"I'm not," said Bob with a wider smile. "I'm not giving up at all. I'm making every moment count, as I have always done."

Roger wiped a tear as he looked around the room that looked too empty with only one small bouquet of flowers on a chest of drawers.

"Maybe I should let you rest," Roger said. "Are you tired?"

"No," said Bob, "there's plenty of time for rest. Let's get down to business."

"What do you mean?" Roger asked.

"What do I mean?" Bob said, pretending to frown. "You forget so easily? It's Monday! We have an appointment!"

"Oh, that!" Roger said. "We can do it some other time. I don't think it's a good idea for you to exert yourself."

"Nonsense," Bob stated. "There's no time like the present. Let's see . . ."

Bob paused and closed his eyes a moment. Roger thought he had gone back to sleep.

"Ah, yes!" Bob said, opening his eyes again. "We finally got to the last of Alice's directives."

"Yes," said Roger. "Directive Six."

"Did you bring your notebook?" Bob asked.

"Yes," said Roger, taking out his orange notebook. "Do you want me to get yours?"

"No need," replied Bob. "I know this one by heart."

Bob looked at Roger with surprising intensity and held out his hand. Roger took it in his. Bob's hand felt light, like silky paper. Bob gave Roger's hand a faint squeeze.

Directive 6:
Leave a legacy.

"Leave a legacy," Bob said and paused to breathe again, letting his head sink back into the pillow.

"Leave a legacy." Roger nodded.

"Leave a legacy," Bob repeated between long breaths. "Don't just take from the past."

Roger waited for Bob to continue. Bob smiled and closed his eyes again. His breathing became shallower, and his hand relaxed as if he were falling asleep again. Roger turned off the bed light, while still holding his hand, and stayed there, praying. He lost track of time, listening to Bob inhaling and exhaling ever so faintly. The door opened silently, and the nurse came in to check on Bob.

Roger retreated from the bed while the nurse carefully did her routine. He wrote in his little orange notebook: *Directive Six: Leave a legacy (don't just take from the past).* Roger looked at his watch—Bob's gold watch—and sighed. He read again from his notes in the little orange notebook. So much had happened since he met Bob. It almost didn't seem real that his marriage to Darlene had been on a hopeless downward slide. He now felt closer to Darlene than ever before. Becca and Sarah, his neighbor Andrew, his client Barton—they all seemed connected by an invisible thread now, made better, made happier, given more hope, all thanks to Bob.

Roger left Bob to rest. Just as he closed the door behind him, a handsome young man approached.

"Are you Roger, by any chance?" he asked.

"Yes, I am," Roger said with surprise.

"I'm Bob's son-in-law," the young man said with a chuckle. "Bob told us you might be coming. He said you two had an appointment for a meeting of some sort. He pretty much ordered us to clear out."

"Is that right?" Roger smiled and looked back toward the door to Bob's room. "Well, we did in fact have our meeting. I just talked to him for a few minutes until he fell asleep."

"I'm glad you made it," said the man simply.

"To tell you the truth," Roger said, "I confess that I was wondering why Bob was by himself. And the room seemed so empty."

"Oh, that!" The son-in-law explained, "Bob got so many flowers that he had the nurses distribute them to all the other rooms. I think pretty much every patient in the entire hospital got a bouquet!"

"I should have known!" Roger laughed.

The rest of the family started to fill the waiting room and gather around Roger. As the hours passed, more people arrived. They all talked and shared stories; some gathered to pray together. Roger was reluctant to leave, as if his presence there was to contribute to Bob's vital signs, to give him strength.

On the drive back home, Roger kept going over his conversations with Bob, all the way back to that first evening when he had heard Bob singing in the corridor, belting out the aria at the top of his voice. As he pulled into his driveway, Roger was glad to see the lights were still on in the kitchen. Darlene must be waiting up. The words of the aria that Bob had been singing resonated again. *No one sleeps. No one sleeps.*

The following morning, Roger decided to stop by the hospital to pay a visit to Bob before going to work. He was surprised to find the patient sitting up in bed and chattering happily with a nurse.

"There you are!" Bob chirped. "I was hoping you'd visit me today!"

Roger settled in the chair by the side of the bed and waited as the nurse went through her motions of checking and arranging the tubes and needles that now formed part of Bob's system of support. Roger observed with relief that Bob's cheeks had some color and that his breath was not half as labored as the day before. An open Bible and Bob's little orange notebook lay on the small bedside table, together with a stack of cut colored paper, obviously an art project from one of Bob's grandchildren.

"How are you feeling today?" Roger asked.

"Like somebody just tossed me into the spin cycle of an industrial washer," Bob quipped. "I'm almost surprised that I'm still here."

Roger looked up at Bob's eyes. He saw a watery, clear gaze, somewhat tired, but there was no fear.

"I hope you don't mean that," Roger said softly. "You have many good years ahead of you."

"It's not the length of years that's important, is it?" Bob said, pushing down on the bed to prop himself up.

Roger fluffed up the pillow behind him, and Bob leaned back and smiled.

"I mean, it's not the number of years," Bob continued, "but what you do with them that counts."

"But surely everybody wants to live a long life," Roger said.

"Naturally," Bob said, "because somehow we have been taught to think that the worth of our lives can be counted in numbers. But in the end we are all given an amount of time, shorter or longer, to do something with. When you look at a graveyard, what do you see?"

"Gravestones?" Roger said.

"And what do they usually say?" Bob asked.

"Well, they sometimes have a verse from Scripture," Roger answered.

"Sure, but even before that, they have the dates, don't they?" Bob said. "They usually say John Smith, 1939 through 1987 . . . as if those dates were the most important thing that should be known about the person whose remains are laid to rest there."

"And why do I suspect that you don't think they are the most important thing?" Roger asked.

"Of course I don't!" Bob gently smacked Roger's upper arm. "This is what I think. Imagine you are looking at John Smith's gravestone. Forget the two dates. Just concentrate on the space between the two. What happened there? What did that life contribute? After the second date formed the final bookend of that person's time on this earth, what was left behind?"

Bob paused as the nurse came in with his breakfast tray. Roger helped bring the rolling bed table up and adjust it to the proper height. Bob was rapidly gaining color, and his eyes recovered a hint of their usual spark. As soon as the nurse left the room, Bob continued, ignoring the toast and jam and cup of tea on his table.

"Do you see what I am trying to get at?" Bob said. "It doesn't matter if you live two thousand years or twenty. What matters is how you fill the space between the dates on your gravestone."

"It reminds me of Alice's sixth directive," Roger said. "Is that what she meant by *leave a legacy*?"

"You got it!" Bob smiled and tucked into his first piece of toast.

Roger reflected for a moment as he watched Bob become more animated. He still felt this tight fist in his chest, a deep fear of losing his dear friend, a longing to hang on to Bob, even if it was for one more day. Now he was beginning to wonder whether Bob was trying to say something that would make it easier for Roger to say good-bye. Was he really saying good-bye? Roger felt his throat tighten. He blinked rapidly to stop the sudden sting in his eyes.

"Are you going mushy on me?" Bob teased between mouthfuls.

"Nonsense," Roger said. "Just a bit of a cold maybe. Anyway, you look so much better today, and I am so happy to see you getting better."

"The truth is that I am ready whenever my time comes, Roger," Bob stated. "You shouldn't feel sad for me, and you should definitely not feel sad for yourself. We share something that most people don't know in their lifetimes. I've had a full life, I've had friends and love and a wonderful, interesting, career, and what's even better, I got to share some thoughts that have helped other people find their own way. I couldn't ask for more."

"Why does it sound like you are saying good-bye?" Roger said, swallowing hard.

"Because I am," Bob said simply.

"Well," said Roger, shaking his head, "you may be ready to say good-bye, but I am definitely not!"

"You haven't filled your space yet," Bob said.

Roger looked confused.

"The space between your dates," Bob explained. "You haven't filled it yet. That's why you are not ready. I'm ahead of you. If you knew how it felt, you wouldn't be sad."

"How does it feel?" Roger asked.

"How can I explain it?" Bob thought a moment. "Think of a day lately when you've had an active, beautiful day outdoors with your family, and maybe your friends, and you all had a great time."

"Actually, it was just the other day," Roger said, "on Saturday. First I spent some time talking to my neighbor Andrew. I told you about him. He was doing great. I shared one of Alice's directives, and we are meeting again next week. Then I went back home and did some work in the garden and started a barbecue. My client Barton stopped by and had lunch with us. He said that his company would keep doing business with us, and he said such kind words about my company and me. Then afterward we played all afternoon with the girls, and we rode our bikes to the park."

"Were you tired at the end of the day?" Bob asked.

"I was completely exhausted," Roger said, "but happy."

"Precisely," Bob said. "Do you know that feeling you had after you took a shower, just before getting into bed at night, the memories of the wonderful day flashing back inside your memory, your body tired but knowing that your rest is coming? You know that indescribable feeling of well-being?"

Roger nodded, understanding.

"That's how you feel when you have fulfilled your legacy," Bob said, "and that's how I feel now. I am ready. I am tired and happy, and my rest is waiting for me. My mind and my heart are so full of love and memories! I can stay and play for a little longer, but I am also welcoming my nice, soft rest in the arms of my beloved."

Roger nodded again but said nothing.

"Do you see now why you shouldn't feel sad for me?" Bob asked.

Roger smiled and squeezed Bob's hand as a beeping alarm went off in one of the monitors next to the head of the bed. The nurse came in quickly, and Roger got up to make space for her to work. A second nurse almost bumped into

Roger as he left the room. The whole activity around Bob's room changed, and Roger left the hospital with a feeling he could only describe as a strong fist that kept tightly pressing into the pit of his stomach. He returned in the afternoon, but Bob had been moved to the intensive-care unit where visits were restricted. The day after, and then the day after that, Roger joined Bob's family as they prayed and waited.

One night, after a long vigil at the hospital, Roger slid into bed exhausted and fell asleep thinking that Bob was one of the few people whom he had allowed to become really close to him. Roger had a wide circle of friends, work colleagues, family, but in all those relationships he had a tendency to keep his innermost feelings or thoughts to himself. He couldn't think of any person, other than his wife, Darlene, who had so directly looked into his heart as Bob.

Roger had a vivid dream. He saw himself standing at a pier packed with a multitude of people waving white handkerchiefs. A majestic cruise liner was docked at the pier, and at the top deck, Roger could see Bob leaning on the railing and smiling gently at the cheering crowd. With one long blow of the horn, the vessel slowly pushed from the dock and then glided away with gathering speed as it sailed into an amber and turquoise horizon.

CHAPTER FIFTEEN

The church was the biggest Roger had ever been to, and it was packed to the aisles. The choir was singing one of Bob's favorite arias, and it sounded as if the angels had descended from the heavens just to hear the music. Never quite at ease with public speaking, Roger glanced over his shoulder at the crowd. Darlene pressed a reassuring hand on his elbow. When the music stopped, Roger heard his name being introduced, and he walked silently to the microphone.

"I am speaking to you at the gracious request of Bob's family," Roger began, "and I should first say that, although many of you have known Bob most of your lives, I enjoyed his friendship for only the thinnest sliver of time."

Roger glanced over at Darlene and his two little girls. They were smiling at him, eyes brimming with love and pride.

"But although I knew him for a short time, we established a deep connection. I met Bob at a time when I had lost my way. Just like a traveler in a storm, I kept fumbling around, only to find myself veering farther and farther away from the road I was supposed to be on. Like a true friend, Bob shared his inner compass with me and pointed me in the true direction. Not just from his personal experience, but back to the source of true direction, Jesus Christ. Almost immediately I started to find my footing again. The experience has enriched not only my life but also the lives of my family and my business associates and my friends. Bob took time to talk to me and share some of his extraordinary wisdom. He said that he owed this wisdom and knowledge to Alice, his beloved wife, and to his relationship with God. I can only imagine how many lost travelers like me Bob has helped find their true north. I believe some of you may even be here today, and you may know what I mean when I say, 'God bless you, Bob, for those six directives.'"

A timid hand went up in the back of the church. Roger looked up and recognized the smiling face of his neighbor Andrew. Then another hand went up, then another and another. Suddenly what looked like hundreds of hands went up in acknowledgment. A breeze of gentle laughter wafted through the congregation.

"Bob took the time to explain in detail each one of these lessons, except the last. Bob barely had the time to share with me the words of the last directive. He left us before he could explain. How would I ever understand this without his wise guidance? It didn't take me very long to realize that the explanation was all around me. As I look at all of you today, coming together to recognize the life of this man, the meaning of his last directive has become clearer than any words could ever make it. Because in each hand that was raised, in each life that was touched, Bob's wisdom lives and multiplies. Each one of those hands will hold even more hands through the thick of despair and into a brighter future. So that is why I say that I can now perfectly understand the meaning of Bob's last directive: *leave a legacy*. I can understand it because I am looking at it.

"Bob once told me that his goal was to someday hear God say to him, as it relates to the life he lived, 'Well done, good and faithful servant!' From the evidence here in this room, I believe Bob has personally heard those words. What an eternally significant goal to achieve and a legacy to leave."

EPILOGUE

I'm leaving for the day," Becky said, sticking her head through the open office door. Roger was talking with Barton Woods. Becky added, "This package came for you."

"Thank-you, Becky," said Roger. "Have a good weekend."

Barton waited as Roger opened the thick padded envelope to reveal a letter and a black leather box.

"It's from Bob's family," said Roger, reading the note. "It says he wanted me to have it."

"The watch?" Barton asked.

"I returned it to the family after the service." Roger nodded. "But the note says they all agreed that it now belongs to me."

"That's quite an honor!" Barton said. "They sound like a fine bunch of people. I'm just sorry I never got to meet Bob."

"Yes," said Roger, "you would have enjoyed talking to him."

"But I'm still getting his six directives through you." Barton winked. "In a way I feel like I know him a little."

Roger smiled as he opened the black box to reveal the familiar object with its inscription.

Pass it around.

ACKNOWLEDGMENTS

—from Todd Hopkins

Doris Michaels with DSM Agency in New York. Wow, you are the best!

Our creative writer, Sylvia Edwards Davis. You bring it all to life!

Jeffrey Fox, for believing in this book enough to hand it to the right people.

Victor Oliver and Paula Major and everyone at Thomas Nelson Publishers, for all the hard work that has gone into the publishing of this book.

Verne Harnish, for your early endorsement and enthusiasm that this was a message many business leaders needed to read.

All the Janitor Bobs in the world, who provide the inspiration behind the story.

All the CEOs and business leaders living out this message every day.

My Office Pride franchise family and corporate staff, for being so good that I can take time to write.

My wife, Michelle, with whom I share life.

My sons, James, Sam, and Matthew. You guys are the greatest. God is going to use you in a great way.

My dad and mom, James and Sheila Hopkins, for supporting me in everything I do.

My pastor, John Spencer, at Calvary Chapel, who teaches the Word of God faithfully, and from whom I have learned so much.

All my CBMC brothers from around the world, who have prayed for me and taught me so much.

My peers in BSCAI, who have helped me grow and who understand how real to life this story is.

Ray Hilbert. It has been a blast to work on this project with you. Thanks for teaching people in our organization how to find purpose to their work.

My friends, Bill Lewis, John McBeath, and Blake Clements, who provided early feedback and good ideas that helped make this book better.

Finally, and most important, my Lord and Savior, Jesus Christ. Through Him all things are possible.

—from Ray Hilbert

First and foremost, thank-You, Lord Jesus—I would be lost without You! You are everything to me.

To my bride and life partner, Beth—thank-you! You have

loved me well—I only pray that I can always be the husband you desire and deserve.

To my children Andrew, Mackenzie, and Brooke—I pray you can truly understand how much your dad loves you—throughout your lives, seek the Lord with all your heart; keep your word; live with integrity; follow your dreams; and always live and love with passion!

Thank-you to Doris Michaels at the DSM Agency for believing in this book project. Your support has been incredible.

Special thanks to our friends at Thomas Nelson Publishers for working with us so diligently on this book.

Todd Hopkins—you are a dear friend and true inspiration—thank-you for allowing me to partner with you on this incredible project! I am so grateful you are in my life.

Thank-you, Bob Blume—for building into me as a young boy—I am eternally grateful!

To my high school baseball coach, Bob Stecher—thank-you for being my *Janitor Bob*.

To the entire Bates family for helping me in my college years in ways that go beyond words.

Mom and Dad—thank-you for loving me enough to teach me the value of a strong work ethic.

Matt Peelen—thank-you for your faithful friendship and partnering with me when Truth@Work was just an idea on a piece of paper—wow, we have come a long way!

ACKNOWLEDGMENTS

Bob Haddad—the most loyal and faithful friend a guy could ever have—I love you, bro!

Perry Hines—you are awesome, my friend, and I am so glad you are part of my life.

To every member (past, present, and future) of Truth @Work—thank-you for your dedication and commitment to living out your faith in the marketplace—you are making a difference in the world!

Buck Jacobs—thank-you for all you taught me about ministry in the marketplace—you are a true pioneer.

Tom Dafnos and the board of directors of Truth@Work—thank-you for your support and encouragement and for allowing me the freedom to write.

Thank-you—the reader of this book—for allowing Janitor Bob Tidwell to impact your life and the lives of others.

Pass it around.

ABOUT THE AUTHORS

Todd Hopkins is the founder and CEO of Office Pride Commercial Cleaning Services, a multimillion-dollar janitorial franchising company with its corporate office in Franklin, Indiana. Founded in 1992, Office Pride now has more than one hundred franchise locations throughout the United States and provides cleaning services to thousands of buildings. Office Pride's goal is to become the *most admired* commercial cleaning service in the world.

Todd is one of the most sought-after speakers in the building service contracting industry. He has spoken nationally on such topics as Entrepreneurial Survival, Sales Success, Employee Motivation and Training, Effective Employee Communications, Customer Service and Retention, and Growing a Business to the Next Level. He is very involved with the Building Service Contractors Association International, the industry's top association, and has served on its board of directors. His industry travels take him throughout the USA and into other countries, such as Brazil, Mexico, and South Korea.

Todd earned his BBA degree from the University of Memphis and his MBA from Butler University. Todd is also a graduate of the MIT Birthing of Giants Executive Entrepreneur Leadership program. He has been involved in many community organizations and was recognized in the "40 under 40 for Indianapolis," which each year honors forty community and business leaders who, before the age of forty, have had a significant impact on the city of Indianapolis.

Todd is an active speaker at business events and Christian outreaches. He is a firm believer that one should never stop learning. Through CBMC (Connecting Businessmen to Christ) and Truth@Work, Todd is involved in Bible study groups aimed at helping to equip business leaders to live and share the good news of Jesus Christ in the marketplace.

Todd and his wife, Michelle, have three boys, James, Sam, and Matthew. They live in Pensacola, Florida, and attend Calvary Chapel Gulf Breeze.

Ray Hilbert is becoming known across the nation for his entertaining, straightforward, and challenging talks to leaders. Applying leadership and life lessons learned through his experiences at major corporate and nonprofit organizations, Ray's passion is "to equip, encourage, challenge, and motivate others to be all they can be to the glory of God." In other words, his *why* is to help others discover and fulfill their *why*. Wherever he speaks, people consistently make important decisions about their work and career, dedicating themselves to living lives of personal integrity and excellence.

In 1998, Ray became the cofounder and CEO of Truth @Work, a not-for-profit organization based in Indianapolis, Indiana. Truth@Work specializes in developing products, programs, and services that help Christian business owners and marketplace leaders integrate their faith into their daily work. Ray has developed many tools to help Christians build and operate their lives and businesses on proven biblical principles. He travels across America, speaking to organizations and churches, equipping people to serve God in and through their work.

He is also in high demand on the speaking faculty of Orlando, Florida–based Man in the Mirror, traveling nationally, delivering workshops, retreats, and seminars.

From 1993 to 1998, Ray was a regional director for Promise Keepers, the nationally known men's ministry, where he facilitated large conferences of sixty thousand and developed training programs for churches and other ministries.

He is a graduate of Anderson University in Anderson, Indiana, where he majored in marketing and business.

In the 1980s and early 1990s, Ray worked with some of America's top corporations where he developed many training seminars and workshops for organizations in the manufacturing, education, and health-care industries.

ABOUT THE AUTHORS

While in college, Ray excelled in baseball and in 1986 traveled throughout America and Asia with the USA Athletes in Action team. He currently enjoys golf and spending time with his family.

Ray and his wife, Beth, reside in Indianapolis with their son and two daughters. They are heavily involved in their local church and with several other religious and business organizations.

Todd and Ray hope that you enjoyed reading *The Janitor* as much as they did writing it.

The authors would love to hear how reading *The Janitor* has impacted your life.

If you would like to post your thoughts and/or comments on the book, please visit **www.LegacyCoaching.com**.

Todd and Ray also welcome the opportunity to help your church, company, or organization *bring to life* the six directives presented in *The Janitor*. Through specialized keynote presentations, workshops, and seminars, their programs and services train and equip business owners and executives on building and operating their businesses and personal lives according to biblical principles.

Additionally, their company, Legacy Coaching, LLC, features a team of highly qualified professionals, offering coaching and training in a wide variety of topics, including, but not limited to, sales training, leadership and organizational development, and team building as well as personal and executive coaching services.

For more information or to contact Todd and/or Ray, please visit
www.LegacyCoaching.com.

Commit to the LORD whatever you do, and your plans will succeed.
—Proverbs 16:3

The mission of Office Pride Commercial Cleaning Services is to honor and glorify God by building mutually beneficial relationships with customers, employees, vendors, and franchisees and fulfilling our promise of providing top-quality janitorial services through men and women committed to honesty, integrity, and hard work.

Core Beliefs and Values:
- Honor God
- Always Do What Is Right
- Increase Brand Value
- Demonstrate Honesty, Integrity, and a Hard Work Ethic
- Total Customer Satisfaction
- Go the Extra Mile
- Persevere with a Servant's Attitude

For Area Development, Franchise or Other Information, Please Call:
317-738-9280

The mission of Truth@Work is to change the way America works by bringing the good news of Jesus Christ to the marketplace.

Truth@Work equips today's leaders to impact the marketplace for Christ.

To contact Ray Hilbert and find out more about how Truth@Work helps Christian business owners and leaders, please call:

317-842-1694

or visit